Snooker Legends

Steve Davis and Dennis Taylor with Nick Hunter (BBC Sports Producer). The 1985 World Championship Final attracted 18.5 million viewers, the final black not being potted until 12.23 a.m. (© BBC)

Snooker Legends

DEAN P. HAYES

FOREWORD BY
TERRY GRIFFITHS

SUTTON PUBLISHING

First published in 2004 by
Sutton Publishing, an imprint of
NPI Media Group · Cirencester Road
Chalford · Stroud · Gloucestershire · GL6 8PE

Reprinted 2005, 2007

British Library Cataloguing in Publication Data
A catalogue record for this book is available from the
British Library.

ISBN 978-0-7509-3233-2

Typeset in 10.5/13.5 Photina.
Typesetting and origination by
Sutton Publishing.
Printed and bound in England.

Contents

Foreword

It is clear that snooker today, having moved into the twenty-first century, has never faced a more challenging but exciting future. With the game growing all the time, especially overseas, there is more pressure than ever on the professional players. The standard of play today is such that any one of the top 100 players can beat each other, while in my day only about a dozen were capable of doing so. As the rewards for success have risen dramatically over the years, and as media coverage has mushroomed, a more heady and hectic lifestyle has become inevitable for those still playing on the circuit.

All this has its place, but it is important not to lose touch with the grass roots of the game. In my case, although I have been lucky enough to travel all over the globe in my career, and despite having won the World Championship at my first attempt in 1979, going on over the years to win numerous other titles, including the Coral UK Championship (beating Alex Higgins 16–15 in the final), I still feel at home in my own snooker club in my home town of Llanelli, both watching and playing against the members. Furthermore, I have never tired of playing and practising during my many years of competition.

I last played at the top in 1997 when I lost 10–9 to Mark Williams in the World Championship at the Crucible. Since then I have continued to be an avid watcher of the game as well as coach to a number of the game's top stars.

For me, snooker is the greatest sport in the world. I very much hope that this informative and entertaining book, written by Dean Hayes, will inspire you with all the enthusiasm that I have for this great game.

Terry Griffiths

Introduction

Over the last few decades, the game of snooker has emerged from relative obscurity to become one of the most popular of all pastimes, enjoyed by players and spectators alike. Some of the credit for this must go to television companies, whose excellent coverage of the major snooker tournaments has brought this colourful game into homes up and down the country and to an audience who have generally never lifted a cue. But the snooker circuit is by no means a media invention: the game has a history, with elegant conventions, its own legendary figures and innumerable famous incidents.

It is now widely accepted that snooker originated in Jubbolpore, India, in 1875. A group of army officers, including a young subaltern named Sir Neville Chamberlain, were playing black pool on the mess billiards table. To add variety, other coloured balls were added and given different scoring values. Sir Neville, observing that one of his opponents had failed to pot a ball and had left him an unplayable shot, accused him of being 'a regular snooker'. At that time, a 'snooker' was the nickname for a first-year cadet at the Woolwich Military Academy. Thus snooker, the game, was christened.

Before long, rumours of this 'new' game reached England, and a well-known professional billiards player, John Roberts, travelled to Calcutta to discover the rules. The game caught on rapidly and by 1927 Joe Davis, a player who was to become a household name in many parts of the world, had organized the first world professional championship, which he won. Davis was in a class of his own in those days, winning the world title every year until 1940, when the event was suspended because of the Second World War. He resumed his run of success after the war, winning the title once more in 1946 before retiring undefeated.

The war years, as in so many areas of sports development, helped snooker gain popularity among the working classes. Tables were set up in army messes and public houses, and the game was played and enjoyed by servicemen on leave or during off-duty periods in their barracks. After the war the game continued to prosper – although it was not until television took an interest that players were able to make such a handsome living from the professional game.

Evaluating greatness in snooker, as in any other sport, is, of course, a subjective business and we will all have our own ideas as to who should qualify as a legend. What criteria should we use to decide? Should we choose the most skilful, the most popular with the fans, or those who won the most tournaments? The parameters are endless. Finally, I opted not necessarily for the most talented players but rather for those who have made a major contribution to the history of the game. I have to confess that my selection is biased towards players who were in their prime during my formative years. I make no apology for that; we all tend to remember with special affection those at their peak during such a time in our lives.

Few will dispute the contribution made to the game by Joe Davis, Ray Reardon, Steve Davis and Stephen Hendry – all names that have become synonymous with the sport of snooker. Other players in this book may not have scaled the same heights but each created his own niche within the sport. As for those not included, the debate and strong feelings engendered by their omission is perhaps the most eloquent testimony there could be to their own contribution to this great game.

Dean P. Hayes
Pembrokeshire
2004

The Legends

Eddie Charlton

Born: 31 October 1929, Merewether, New South Wales, Australia

Career highlights
Pot Black Champion 1972, 1973, 1980
World Matchplay Champion 1976
Limosin International Champion 1979

THROUGHOUT HIS CAREER, Eddie Charlton has been one of the game's greatest servants, spending his life globetrotting to spread the snooker word. He has played in more than twenty-five countries, including exotic spots such as Papua New Guinea, China, Japan and Hong Kong, and has made the journey between Sydney and London more than 100 times.

Eddie has lived most of his life in Swansea, a coalmining and fishing area about ninety miles north of Sydney where his grandfather had a small three-table billiard saloon. He began playing snooker when he was 9 and in 1940, when Eddie was 11, the great Walter Lindrum (uncle of Horace), having heard of his prowess, wrote to his grandfather asking him to bring Eddie to Sydney to play an exhibition game. The invitation was accepted and Eddie played Walter one afternoon before a crowd of approximately 600 people.

He made his first century break at 17, but spent much of his youth, with some success, playing more robust sports. These included ten years of first-grade soccer, participating in the 1950 Australian Surfing Championship with the Swansea Belmont crew, a string of victories in speed roller-skating, and spells of competitive cricket, athletics, boxing and tennis. He was also one of the carriers of the Olympic torch for the 1956 Olympics in Melbourne – a memory he cherishes as one of the most exciting moments of his sporting career – and boxed an exhibition bout with Dave Sands, then world middleweight champion.

Following his exhibition game against Walter Lindrum, Eddie continued his education at his local secondary school in Swansea and then became a trainee apprentice fitter in the coalmining industry. He turned professional in 1960 when he was still a miner and gradually began to concentrate on what was, after all, his number-one game. As an amateur, he had won three New South Wales state snooker titles and one New South Wales billiards title.

Charlton first visited England in 1968 to challenge John Pulman for the world title. In those days the champion defended his title against any

challenger who could make a satisfactory commercial offer. He was beaten 39–34 and did not play in the championship again until 1970, when it was held in Australia. That year, and again in 1972, he was beaten in the semi-finals, though in the latter he pushed John Spencer hard, eventually losing 37–32. The highlight of his 1972 trip was winning the first of two consecutive *Pot Black* titles, a success that may have been instrumental in the Australian Broadcasting Corporation's decision to buy the series. Charlton, in fact, holds the break record for the BBC TV series – his break of 110 in 1973 was never bettered. He certainly liked the 'quick-fire' format of the *Pot Black* series, winning the event on three occasions and finishing runner-up once.

Though he came close on a number of occasions, Charlton never won the world title. He led Ray Reardon 7–0 in the 1973 World Championship Final but lost 38–32. Two years later he led Reardon 28–23 but was beaten 31–30. In 1976 he lost to Alex Higgins in the semi-finals and later unsuccessfully challenged Rex Williams for the World Billiards title. At Sheffield in the 1977 World Championship, he met the Canadian champion Cliff Thorburn in the quarter-finals but lost by one frame, 13–12. Twelve months later the same two players met again in the quarter-finals, the result and score on that occasion being reversed, with Eddie beating Cliff by one frame. However, Eddie's hopes of reaching the final disappeared when Ray Reardon beat him 18–14 in the semi-finals. Charlton reached the semi-finals again in 1979, only to lose to the eventual winner, Terry Griffiths. Consolation for Eddie followed when he beat John Virgo in the 13-frame play-off for third place.

Outside the World Championship, Charlton's successes have included a 31–24 defeat of Reardon in the final of the controversial 1976 World Matchplay Championship in Melbourne and a 23–19 defeat of John Spencer in the final of the biggest tournament in South Africa, the Limosin International in Cape Town in 1979.

The 1987–8 season held a number of proud moments for Charlton, on both a personal and a professional level. He already had three grown-up children from a previous marriage, but he became a father again at the age of 57, when his wife Robyn presented him with a son, Andrew. He also helped Australia reach the final of the Fersina World Cup in Bournemouth, a tournament in which eight teams of three players play on a knockout basis. England was the red-hot favourite, but with the score at 1–1 Charlton beat Jimmy White 3–1. The proud Aussie looked like causing one of the upsets of the season, but Steve Davis ruined Eddie's day, winning the last four frames of the competition, two against Eddie and two against Warren King, to give England the trophy by a 9–7 margin.

Charlton's snooker activities extended beyond the table. He was involved with coaching and promoting and took his highly successful 'Snooker Circus' around Australia. As a promoter he was involved in the 1970 and 1975 World Snooker Championships held in Australia and also in the 1974 and 1976 World Professional Billiards Championships. The Eddie Charlton 'Snooker Circus' gave the people of Australia an opportunity to watch live snooker that they would not otherwise have had. Charlton, his son Edward and brother Jim (who were both also professional players) and Australian professional Ian Anderson would set off around the country in a large truck containing a snooker table, accessories and banked seating accommodation for 500. On reaching their venue, generally in some obscure backwater, they would set this up with the help of Jim's son Garth and treat members of the public to an exhibition of top-class snooker skills.

While other players came and went, 'Steady Eddie', as he was known on the circuit, just kept plugging away, throughout his career, his competitive instinct never swaying. With a cue action as straight as a gun barrel, he was one of the game's cleanest and most consistent potters, but his unwillingness to use side-spin for fear of endangering the certainty of the immediate pot demonstrated the conservative side of his nature, one that may have contributed to his losing a number of close matches that a more positive player might have won.

Charlton retired from the demands of professional snooker at the end of the 1994–5 season, but the strongly built Aussie is still a keep-fit fanatic and tries to go out for a jog every day. Awarded the Australian Order of Merit for his services to the sport, Charlton, now sporting a new hairpiece, is currently active in promoting the game of pool, which is taking off in a big way Down Under.

Fred Davis

Born: 14 August 1913, Whittingham Moor, Chesterfield
Died: 15 April 1998

Career highlights
World Professional Snooker Champion 1948, 1949, 1951

UK Professional Billiards Champion 1951
Professional Matchplay Snooker Champion 1952, 1953, 1954, 1955, 1956
News of the World Champion 1958, 1959
Australian Open Champion 1960
World Professional Billiards Champion 1980

DESPITE WINNING the World Championship in eight out of ten appearances in the final – the earliest being in 1940 and the last in 1966 – the lovable Fred Davis had to endure living in older brother Joe's shadow throughout his prime years.

Some twelve years the younger, Fred began playing on a miniature table at his home on Whittingham Moor near Chesterfield. No one so much as told him the rules of the game but he picked up the basics very quickly. His brother Joe dismissed him as neither dedicated nor ambitious enough, offering little advice and certainly no coaching to his younger sibling. But, because he was working in the family's billiard hall in Chesterfield, Fred really had no alternative but to become a professional on his sixteenth birthday, although brother Joe, still somewhat dismissive of his talent, discouraged him from entering the Junior Professional Billiards Championship. In fact, Fred won the event on each of the three occasions it was held.

Short sight was a big problem for Fred, the wearing of spectacles making the game difficult for him. His solution was to introduce the famous swivel-lens spectacles that subsequently became the saviour of many short-sighted snooker players.

In his first World Snooker Championship in 1937 Fred lost 17–14 to Welshman Bill Withers, though family pride was restored when Joe defeated Withers 30–1 in the next round of the competition. Joe and Fred met in the World Final just once, in 1940, the pair of them treating the spectators to one of the greatest matches of all time. Joe won, but only by a single frame in a best-of-73-frames match. Outside the World Championship, the two played some equally memorable matches. Joe preferred to concede a black start, a handicap that hardly reduced his chances of winning but safeguarded his reputation and record should he lose. Nevertheless, on four

occasions Fred defeated Joe on level terms, the only player ever to do so. His first victory over Joe was in the *Empire News* Tournament, a round-robin event, with each match lasting a week, which ran through the 1948–9 season at Leicester Square Hall. Fred won 36–35, but the tournament had been conducted on a sealed handicap basis and when this revealed Fred to be conceding a two-frame start Joe was presented with a 37–36 victory. This not only obscured Fred's feat but gave Joe the first prize of £450. The second victory, 37–34, occurred in a week's challenge match, again at Leicester Square Hall, in 1949. The third, 20–17, came in a three-day match on level terms in the *News of the World* Tournament in 1952, and the fourth victory of 21–16 was again in the *News of the World* Tournament, this time in 1954.

Fred subsequently spent over five years away from the sport serving with the army during the Second World War, but in 1947, after Joe's retirement from serious competition, he had a golden opportunity to replace his brother as world champion. Up against Scotsman Walter Donaldson, he started as favourite, but Donaldson, having practised in his loft for weeks on end, showed real fighting spirit and Davis could not break through. Consequently, for the first time since the introduction of the championship in 1927, a member of the Davis family was not world champion that year. Fred made amends in 1948, avenging his defeat against Donaldson to take the title. He beat the same player again in 1949 and then in 1951, 1952 and 1953; a slight hiccup in 1950 led to Donaldson taking the title back, albeit temporarily. Walter Donaldson's retirement in 1954 led to Fred meeting John Pulman in the 1955 and 1956 World Finals. Fred saw him off as well, the narrow victories in each match completing his eight-title haul.

Public interest in the game, however, was diminishing at this time, not least due to the failure of new names to break into the world of professional snooker. There was still a living to be earned from the club exhibition circuit but this could hardly be called competitive sport. In consequence, Fred decided to curtail his twenty-year professional career and retire to his wife's Llandudno hotel. He returned from exile in 1964, just as the game was beginning to stir itself again, but the edge had gone from his play and he was beaten by Pulman three times in head-to-head challenge matches for the world title. The revival of a proper knockout tournament served to whet Fred's appetite for the game, but he found life much tougher against the new breed of professionals. Then in 1970 Fred suffered the first of two heart attacks and was able to play in only one of the two World Championships that were held that year. Four years later, however, after another bout of ill health, he quite amazingly won the last three frames against Alex 'Hurricane' Higgins to edge into the 1974 quarter-finals by 15 frames to 14. Sadly Fred's stamina was evidently not what it had once been, and,

Steve Davis and Fred Davis.

exhausted by his efforts, he lost to Ray Reardon in the semi-finals.

In 1977 Fred was awarded the OBE for his services to snooker. This made a unique snooker 'double', as his brother Joe had also been awarded the OBE some years earlier.

Back in the championship for the 1978 world title, Fred was in excellent form. By now wearing contact lenses instead of his famous 'swivel-lens', he beat Dennis Taylor and then the UK Professional Champion Patsy Fagan. This took him into the semi-finals, but, in spite of a tremendous display of his old skills, his opponent from South Africa, Perrie Mans, finally won the game by 18 frames to 16.

In recognition of his services to English snooker, Davis was made captain of the England team that competed in the 1979 and 1980 world team championships; he led the team to second place behind Wales in the inaugural competition in 1979.

Even after achieving so much within the sport he still had one ambition left and that was to win the World Billiards title. To his surprise and that of the defending champion Rex Williams, he triumphed in a nail-biting battle over four days to become only the second man after his brother Joe to win the world professional titles at both sports.

Just two days before the start of the 1998 Embassy World Championships, Fred Davis passed away at the age of 84. A universally popular figure who always played the game with a smile on his face, he had continued to compete into his eighties and was always the most sporting of players.

Joe Davis

Born: 15 April 1901, Whitwell, Derbyshire
Died: 10 July 1978

Career highlights
World Professional Snooker Champion 1927, 1928, 1929, 1930, 1931, 1932, 1933, 1934, 1935, 1936, 1937, 1938, 1939, 1940, 1946

World Professional Billiards Champion 1928, 1929, 1930, 1932
UK Professional Billiards Champion 1934, 1935, 1936, 1937, 1938, 1939, 1940, 1946, 1947
Daily Mail Gold Cup Champion 1937, 1938
Empire News Champion 1949
News of the World Champion 1950, 1953, 1956

DUBBED by a *Daily Mail* cartoonist 'the Sultan of Snooker' and 'the Emperor of Pot', Joe Davis was indeed the King. To a certain extent his superiority held back the sport for many years, but without him there would probably not have been a World Championship.

Joe was born at 80 Welbeck Street, Whitwell, Derbyshire – the house still stands today and a plaque commemorates his birth there on 15 April 1901. He was perhaps fortunate that his parents soon moved to The Queens public house at Whittingham Moor near Chesterfield, which housed a full-sized billiards table. Perhaps another fortunate coincidence was that the room had a 3-inch false floor, which allowed Joe to reach the table at a very young age. He made his first billiard century break at 11 years of age, and at 13 he was the Chesterfield and District amateur billiards champion. At 18 he turned professional and in his first professional match he beat Albert Raynor. He figured in his first World Billiards Championship in 1922 but was eliminated by the defending champion, Tom Newman.

It was around this time that Joe Davis's keen interest in snooker was developing and in 1926 he played a significant part in getting the Billiards Association and Control Club to agree to stage a World Snooker Championship. Davis became the first champion in 1927, winning the sum of £6 10s (£6.50 in today's money) for beating Tom Dennis 20–11 in the final held at Camkin's Hall in Birmingham. The title was to remain in Joe Davis's possession until he retired from World Championship play in 1946. In that time he played thirty-four matches in the championship and won them all. The nearest he came to defeat was in the 1940 final when his brother Fred held him to 37–36. The World Billiards title followed the year after his first snooker success, Joe triumphing over Tom Newman, and he went on to win it on four occasions in all. His only defeats in the event were against Walter Lindrum in 1933 and 1934. He was also UK Billiards Champion from

1934 to 1947. His last World Snooker Championship final, in 1946, saw him beat Horace Lindrum, Walter's nephew, in a closely fought match. The result was 78 frames to 67. During this championship, held at London's Royal Horticultural Hall, Joe made a total of six century breaks and raised the championship record break to 136. He subsequently retired from World Professional Championships, but won several other prestigious events, such as the *Daily Mail* Gold Cup, the *Empire News* Tournament and the *News of the World* Tournament. He also continued to play in exhibition matches and handicap events, but, as had happened with John Roberts junior before him, his continued presence in the snooker world inevitably devalued any competition in which he did not participate.

On his retirement from the World Championship scene, many thought Joe should have kept the trophy. Fortunately for the world champions of today, this did not happen. A close circle of friends commissioned an exact replica to be made, and this was presented to Joe in 1949.

Away from the table, Davis was one of the original directors of the new Leicester Square Hall, which was opened in 1947. Like its predecessor, Thurston's, the new hall became the 'home' of snooker. Joe Davis gave some of his best performances there, none better than on 22 January 1955 when, playing Willie Smith, he recorded the first official maximum break of 147. It was as Joe prepared to pot the final black that Ted Lowe, the managing director of the newly refurbished 200-seater billiards and snooker arena, noticed the great man, for the first and only time in his career, exhibiting signs of nerves! Amazingly it took over two years for the break to be ratified by the Billiards Association and Control Council (BACC). The reason for this delay was that, at that time, the professionals had started playing a rule that the BA and CC did not recognize – which stated that a player could make his opponent play again after a foul stroke.

Joe Davis was generally regarded as a plain-ball player, which means he seldom employed side or screw. Little stun shots were usually enough for him to pot the reds and stay around the black spot.

Record breaks constantly fell Joe Davis's way. He made the first of 687 snooker century breaks in Manchester in 1928, aged 27, and though it took him from 1928 to 1939 to make the first 100 of those centuries, it took him a mere two years – from 1953 to 1955 – to move from 500 to 600. He broke the world record snooker break on five occasions: first in 1937 with a break of 137, then in 1938 (138), 1947 (140), 1950 (146) and finally that maximum in 1955. He also broke the World Championship record break several times and, in 1935, compiled the first century in the championship. In billiards he achieved a break of 2,052 against Tom Newman.

A one-time chairman of the Professional Players Association, Joe Davis was also heavily involved with raising money for charity, in recognition of which he was awarded the OBE in 1963. He was delighted to see snooker enter its greatest phase when the World Championship moved to the Crucible Theatre in Sheffield. Ironically, it was while watching his brother Fred's epic World Championship semi-final with Perrie Mans in 1978 that Joe collapsed from the illness that a short while later was to claim his life. He returned to London from Sheffield and subsequently underwent a six-and-a-half-hour operation. Sadly, he never fully recovered, and on 10 July 1978 the man who for a whole generation had embodied everything good about the game passed away while convalescing in Hampshire.

In his will, Davis left nearly £85,000, a small sum compared to what he would have earned from the sport today but large in comparison to the £6.50 he had collected for winning his first world title. He also left his revered cue, which he had bought for just 7s 6d, to his son Derrick, who arranged for it to be displayed at the Eccentrics' Club.

Steve Davis

Born: 22 August 1957, Plumstead, London

Career highlights

Embassy World Champion 1981, 1983, 1984, 1987, 1988, 1989

Coral UK Champion 1980, 1981, 1984, 1985
English Professional Champion 1981
Guinness World of Snooker Champion 1981
Jameson International Champion 1981, 1983, 1984
Yamaha International Champion 1981, 1982, 1984, 1986
Benson & Hedges Masters Champion 1982, 1988
Scottish Masters Champion 1982, 1983, 1984
World Doubles Champion 1982, 1983, 1985, 1986
Benson & Hedges Irish Masters Champion 1983, 1984, 1988, 1997
Lada Classic Champion 1983, 1984
Professional Players Tournament 1983, 1985
British Open Champion 1986, 1993
Tennents UK Champion 1986, 1987
Winfield Masters Champion 1986
Fidelity Unit Trusts International, 1987, 1988, 1989
Mercantile Credit Classic Champion 1987, 1988, 1992
Everest World Matchplay Champion 1988
Rothman's Grand Prix Champion 1988, 1989
Asian Open Champion 1992
European Open Champion 1993
Regal Welsh Champion 1994, 1995

STEVE DAVIS is, in the eyes of many people, the greatest snooker player ever to pick up a cue. Certainly he dominated the 1980s with a skill and authority that made him a sporting superstar and a household name. From being a raw teenager whose only real talent was the ability to play snooker, he developed into one of Britain's finest sporting ambassadors.

Davis began playing snooker in 1969 when he was 12 years old. His father Bill first encouraged him to play while the family were on holiday at a Pontin's holiday camp. A good club player himself with the Plumstead Common Working Men's Club, Bill soon had Steve playing at the club on their return from holiday. In those schoolboy days, Davis used to work on Saturdays to earn some extra pocket money, first in a butcher's shop and then in a greengrocer's. These are the only jobs he has ever had outside his snooker career. He abandoned his A-levels at 17 and left school to play snooker full-time.

Steve's big break came in 1976, by which time he was playing regularly at the Romford Lucania club. In March that year the club was bought by Barry Hearn, who immediately spotted Davis's potential and put him under

contract. The next eighteen months were to see spectacular progress. In August 1977 Steve registered the first maximum break of his career when playing Ray Martin in a practice match at the Plumstead Common Club. He was subsequently selected for the England team in the Home International Championship, won the Working Men's Club and Institute Union snooker title, was narrowly beaten by nine-times winner Norman Dagley in the billiards final, was a member of the winning London team in the Inter-Counties Championship, and went on to beat Tony Meo 7–4 in the final of the Pontin's Open at Prestatyn.

Steve moved up from amateur status in September 1978, and his first win as a professional was a repetition of his Pontin's Open success. This time, instead of receiving 30 points per frame, he was conceding 30, but he still managed to win the title by beating amateur Jimmy White in the final. The first man, though, to feel the real weight of Davis's power was Alex Higgins. The Irishman was beaten 16–6 in the final of the 1980 Coral UK Championship – an event that Davis was to turn into a one-man show during much of the 1980s. Less than a week later Davis won the Wilson Classic at Bolton, beating Dennis Taylor in the final.

Five individual titles and the world team title came Davis's way in 1981, but the most cherished, naturally, was his first world title at the Crucible. He dismissed Jimmy White, Alex Higgins, Terry Griffiths and Canadian Cliff Thorburn on his way to the final, where he beat Doug Mountjoy 18–12.

Davis added four more major individual titles to his list of successes the following year. In addition he won the inaugural world doubles title with Tony Meo and the *Pot Black* and Pontin's Professional titles. He also scored the first 147 ever seen on television at the Lada Classic. But if 1982 brought more honours for Steve Davis, it also brought him one of the biggest shocks of his career – indeed one of the biggest in the history of the sport. Up against new professional Tony Knowles in the first round of his World Championship defence, Davis slumped to a 10–1 defeat. There were also defeats in the final of the Benson & Hedges Irish Masters and the Lada Classic, on both occasions to Terry Griffiths. Not surprisingly, the pundits were all too ready to suggest he was over the hill! The following year, however, he won back his Irish Masters, Jameson International and World Professional titles and also won the Lada, Scottish Masters and Tolly Cobbold Classic, the world doubles for the second year running and the world team title. Having won the latter, Davis simultaneously held all three world professional titles: single, doubles and team.

In 1984 Davis won his third world title when he beat Jimmy White 18–16 in a classic final, the same year also seeing him triumph in the Camus Hong Kong Masters. He came close to winning his third successive world title in 1985 but threw away an 8–0 lead over Dennis Taylor to lose 18–17 to the

Irishman in an epic final that was decided on the last black. Another memorable match involving Steve Davis was the 1987 Mercantile Credit Classic final against Jimmy White. The two were always guaranteed a sell-out crowd, and this time there was also a record ITV audience of 15.2 million who had tuned in to watch the superstars battling it out over twenty-five frames. It was a classic encounter that always looked likely to go the distance, and sure enough just one brilliant snooker settled the outcome of an outstanding game, Davis winning 13–12.

Davis won numerous sporting awards and during his career was awarded the MBE in 1988, followed by the OBE in the Queen's New Year's Honours List of 2002. Fame has naturally brought financial rewards too. He has regularly earned over £1 million a year from his tournament successes and his lucrative sponsorship and advertising contracts; personal appearances have given him a property in the West End of London, a forest in Scotland and an investment portfolio that means he will never have to work again. In demand for all sorts of television programmes, Davis has appeared in advertisements, hosted his own chat show and been the question-master on a quiz show; he is regularly sought after for interviews. Indeed, such was the legend on and off the green baize of Steve 'Interesting' Davis – also known as 'The Nugget' 'The Ginger Mushroom' and 'The Master Cueman' – that he even became the subject of a latex puppet on the satirical television programme *Spitting Image*.

In his illustrious career, Steve has collected seventy-three titles, twenty-eight of them ranking events. One of his last successes came in the Benson & Hedges Irish Masters in 1997 when, following a barren two-year period in which he had failed to add to his long list of major titles, he came from 8–4 behind to beat Ronnie O'Sullivan 10–8. His enthusiasm for the game is as intense as ever and he is eager to win at least one title in the new millennium.

Ken Doherty

Born: 17 September 1969, Dublin, Eire

Career highlights
Embassy World Champion 1997

Scottish Masters Champion 1993, 1994
Regal Welsh Champion 1993, 2001
Dr Marten's European League 1996
Rothman's Grand Prix Champion 2000
Thailand Masters Champion 2001

IN 1997 Ken Doherty, who has a rock-solid all-round game and is known as one of the best tactical players on the circuit, became the first player from the Republic of Ireland to win the world title and the first Irishman since Dennis

Ken Doherty putting pen to paper.

Taylor in 1985. He also became the first player to become world champion at junior, amateur and professional level.

Doherty turned professional in 1991. His prowess as an amateur had promised great things, but, though he reached the televised stage of the World Championship that year, losing 10–8 to Steve Davis in the first round, he had to wait another three years to return to the Crucible. He captured his first ranking tournament in 1993 when he won the Regal Welsh, firmly establishing himself in doing so as part of the elite top sixteen. He also won the 1993 Scottish Masters, repeating the feat the following year. Then, in 1996, Doherty won the Dr Marten's European League and captained the Republic of Ireland at the Castrol–Honda World Cup in Bangkok. There he led by example, defeating England's Ronnie O'Sullivan in the nineteenth and deciding frame to take the Irish team through to the final, where, despite giving favourite Scotland a run for its money, the team lost 10–7.

The highlight of Doherty's career, victory in the 1997 Embassy World Championship final, captivated a nation – RTE, Ireland's national radio and television station, bowed to public pressure and screened the final session between Doherty and Stephen Hendry live, at a stroke reducing the crime rate in Dublin to zero! Doherty's achievement in ending Hendry's 29-match winning streak was remarkable, to say the least. He had been beaten in the first round of the British Open and lost 6–1 to Steve Davis in the Irish Masters. After a titanic struggle against Mark Davis (10–8) in the first round of the Embassy tournament, Doherty beat Steve Davis 13–3, the Romford star's heaviest defeat in the World Championship. He then recovered from losing the first three frames in the quarter-finals against John Higgins to win 13–9 before hammering French-Canadian Alain Robidoux 17–7 in the semi-final. In the final, Doherty led 5–3 after the first session, despite three century breaks from Hendry, and he subsequently extended his lead to 11–5 overnight. In the opening session the next day he stretched his advantage to 15–7 before Hendry mounted a comeback. The Scot won five frames in a row to cut the deficit to 15–12, but, after he had missed a straightforward red in the twenty-eighth frame, the final was effectively over. Ken went on to win 18–12.

After lifting the cherished trophy, which now sits proudly on top of his mother's TV set, Doherty returned to Dublin, where 250,000 people lined the streets to welcome home King Ken as he was driven in an open-top bus round the city. Named Ireland's Sports Personality of the Year for his achievement, he was hailed as 'a fine ambassador and role model for the youth of the country' by the then president Mary Robinson. A Manchester United fanatic, Doherty was able to parade the trophy around the 'Theatre of Dreams' – Old Trafford – on one of his many trips to watch his footballing idols.

No champion has ever successfully defended his first world title at the

Crucible, but Doherty came closer than most in 1998 when he again reached the final. From 10–5 down he fought back to trail John Higgins only 13–11 going into the final session, before the Scot pulled away to win 18–12. Beaten finalist in the Masters at Wembley in both 1999 and 2000, Doherty then came agonizingly close to making a magical maximum in the fifteenth frame of the 2000 final against Matthew Stevens, missing the final black off its spot and thus the chance to drive off with a top-of-the-range Honda sports car worth £80,000.

In 2001 Doherty beat Paul Hunter 9–2 in the final of the Royal Welsh in Cardiff and then Stephen Hendry 9–3 in the final of the Thailand Masters, to make him only the eighth player in snooker history to win back-to-back ranking tournaments. In fact, he was denied a hat-trick only by Peter Ebdon, who ended his fourteen-match winning streak in the final of the Royal Scottish in Aberdeen. In November of the same year, Doherty was beaten 10–1 by Ronnie O'Sullivan in the final of the UK Championship, but two weeks later his marriage to Sarah Prasad in Australia helped him get over the disappointment. In fact, the Dubliner was happy to be playing snooker at all after slipping in his bathroom at home earlier in the season and falling on to

an ornament that pierced his left eyelid just a fraction of an inch above the eyeball.

After losing 10–9 to Mark Williams in a gripping conclusion to the 2002 Powerhouse-sponsored UK Championship at York's Barbican Centre, Doherty was to feature the following year in a gripping World Championship semi-final, producing one of the greatest comebacks in Crucible history to beat Paul Hunter 17–16 and reach the final, where his opponent was again to be Mark Williams. Trailing 15–9 at the start of play on the Saturday, Doherty knew Hunter needed only two frames to win the semi-final, but the Irishman showed amazing nerve to take the first five frames. Both players subsequently made errors as the tension grew, but, after Hunter had moved 16–14 ahead, Doherty dug deep to produce a sensational finish. In the deciding frame, the atmosphere was fraught with nerves but Doherty made brave breaks of 40 and 32 to leave Hunter needing snookers. Revealing afterwards that the memory of his near-collapse against John Higgins in the quarter-final had helped inspire his amazing win – he had seen a 10–0 lead evaporate to 10–7 before he rallied to win 13–8 – he described the match as 'the most incredible game I have ever played in'.

In the final, Doherty produced another amazing comeback, pulling back to 12–12 after being 11–5 behind. With the score at 14–14, Williams edged ahead, and eventually won 18–16. Despite having been taken to the final frame in three of his previous four matches, Doherty refused to blame fatigue for his defeat.

Paying tribute to the Crucible crowd, the Irishman declared, 'It was a great match to be involved in and the atmosphere was absolutely fantastic. This is the best place in the world for snooker and when I was coming back I really thought I would win. I gave it everything. I gave every ball everything and every frame everything. I'm really gutted that I have not won.'

Walter Donaldson

Born: 2 February 1907, Coatbridge, Scotland
Died: 24 May 1973

Career highlights
National Under-16 Billiard Champion 1922
Scottish Professional Billiards Champion 1928
Scottish Professional Snooker Champion 1929, 1930, 1931, 1932, 1937
World Professional Snooker Champion 1947, 1950

ONE OF the original 'grinders', Walter Donaldson was a careful, steady player, but at the same time one of the greatest long-ball potters the game has seen. The first Scottish-born player to join the elite of the snooker world, he won the national Under-16 Billiards Championship in 1922 at the age of 15 and turned professional the following year, going on to win the Scottish Professional Billiards Championship in 1928. Combining hard practice with moves to Rotherham and Chesterfield to manage billiard halls, he began to concentrate on snooker. Unfortunately he was playing in the same era as Joe Davis, and, though able to make a living from the game, he was unable to topple Davis when it came to tournament play. He did, however, enjoy a series of victories in the Scottish Professional Championship.

Donaldson's first venture into world professional snooker championships was in 1933 when he reached the semi-final, only to lose to Davis 13–1. He then went away for no less than six years to work on his game until he re-entered the professional ranks in 1939, the year in which he established himself by finishing fourth in the *Daily Mail* Gold Cup.

After five years' war service in the Eighth Army's desert and Italian campaigns, Donaldson returned home in 1946 to undertake a relentless programme of solo practice to regain his form. The immediate postwar years saw him vying with Fred Davis for the world number-one position, Joe Davis having retired from championship play in 1946, the year that Donaldson established a new official world record break of 142. Fred and Walter met for the first time in the finals of the 1947 World Championship, a confrontation that was to be repeated for the following seven years. The first encounter was at Thurston's, which had now been renamed the Leicester Square Hall after reopening following bomb damage during the war. Even when Donaldson beat Horace Lindrum in the 1947 semi-final, it was still thought by most observers, including Joe, that the name Davis would be engraved on the trophy for the sixteenth time – but they hadn't reckoned with the dour but effective play of the wily Scot. His long potting, in particular, was the most consistently accurate the game had yet seen, this due in large part to his

strict plain ball striking – he would never use side-spin if there was the slightest chance of it compromising his shots. The downside of this orthodox style was that it limited his positional play and restricted the number of centuries he made. Before the final, Donaldson locked himself away with a table in a friend's loft to perfect his long potting, later acknowledged by Davis as some of the finest he had ever witnessed. The result was that Walter triumphed in that first encounter 82–63.

His dour approach and out-thrust determined Scottish chin symbolized his approach to the game and indeed to life. When a friend tried to console him with the words 'Walter, I don't know what to say', after Walter had lost six frames in a row to Fred, his uncompromising reply was: 'Well don't bloody well say anything!'

Donaldson and Davis met again in the final of the 1948 World Championship, which was played at the same venue, the Leicester Square Hall, over 145 frames. This time Fred matched the Scot for safety play, taking no risks and giving few chances – a tactic well illustrated by the fact that there were no century breaks. Davis won 84–61 and both players were honoured by the attendance of the Marquess and Marchioness of Queensberry, plus Joe Davis – there to watch his brother in his hour of victory.

During his semi-final match of the 1949 World Championship against John Pulman, Donaldson made his 100th century break, scoring 100 and 113 in successive frames. In the final, Walter was leading Fred by six frames as late as the eighty-fourth frame but he failed to last the course and Fred came back to take the title in the 131st frame, winning 80–65. It should be pointed out that having to play competitive snooker six hours a day for fourteen days made the game a matter of physical endurance much more than in later tournament play. Donaldson seemed to crack after frame 117; Davis, who was leading 60–57 at the time, went on to win thirteen of the next fourteen frames.

In the 1950 championship, sponsored by *Empire News*, Donaldson's safety play came out on top against a below-par Fred Davis. The game was held at the Tower Gardens in Blackpool and Donaldson won 51–46. The following year, Walter Donaldson beat Horace Lindrum 41–30 in the semi-final, but in the final, again played at the Tower Gardens, Blackpool, and with Donaldson and Davis appearing in the final for the fifth successive time, Davis avenged his previous year's defeat with a convincing 58–39 victory. The crowds exceeded those of any previous year in the history of the event.

In the Matchplay Championship of 1952, which was considered the real snooker championship of the world by the general public, Davis beat Walter Donaldson for the fourth time, 38–35. After Fred had again beaten Walter in 1953 by 37–34 and in 1954 by 39–21, Walter had had enough and retired from the championship. Though an excellent match player, he was not in great demand for exhibitions, and as professional snooker's appeal dwindled he demonstrated his disillusionment with the game by turning the billiard room at his Buckinghamshire home into a cowshed and breaking up the slate of his table to pave a path.

Peter Ebdon

Born: 27 August 1970, Wellingborough, Northamptonshire

Career highlights
Embassy World Champion 2002

Rothman's Grand Prix Champion 1993
Benson & Hedges Irish Masters Champion 1995
Scottish Masters Champion 1996
Thailand Open Champion 1997
British Open Champion 2001
Regal Scottish Champion 2001

ONE OF the game's great showmen, Peter Ebdon – who played the oboe at school and represented London Schools at cricket as a leg-spin bowler – broke his father's heart when he left school after completing his O-levels to pursue a career in snooker, but, like most headstrong teenagers, he knew what was best for him.

Turning professional in 1992, the pony-tailed Ebdon on his first appearance at the Crucible for that year's World Championship beat six-times World Champion Steve Davis 10–4 in his first-round match. He then beat Martin Clark before losing 13–7 to Terry Griffiths in the quarter-finals. Also in his first season, Ebdon made two 147 maximum breaks in the Strachan Challenge and the UK Championship, his achievements that season earning him the WPBSA Young Player of the Year award. He subsequently went from strength to strength, collecting his first ranking title – the Grand Prix – a year later, beating Ken Doherty 9–6 in the final, and following this up in 1995 with victory in the Irish Masters. He twice came close to capturing one of the sport's two top titles, losing 10–3 in the final of the 1995 UK Championship to Stephen Hendry and succumbing to the Scot 18–12 in the final of the 1996 Embassy World Championship. On his way to the latter, Ebdon had defeated Jimmy White, Steve Davis and Ronnie O'Sullivan, but the tight finishes in each of those matches had left him mentally drained. He came back well after a nightmare session on the first day, but was unable to prevent Hendry from collecting his sixth world title. 'I had a very tough draw,' he said, 'and having produced all that effort just to get to the final there was nothing left. But it was a privilege just to play Stephen, because he is the greatest player ever to have picked up a cue.'

That was one of four finals he lost during the 1995–6 season but then he started the 1996–7 campaign with two successes: one in the Regal Scottish Masters, beating Alan McManus 9–6 in the final, and then in the Thailand

Open, where he beat Nigel Bond 9–7. However, after he had established himself as one of the game's leading players, there followed a couple of lean seasons in which Ebdon slipped down the world rankings, though he did make it to the quarter-finals of the 1998 World Championship, only to lose in a thriller, 13–11, to Mark Williams. He re-established himself as a major force in snooker during the 2000–1 season, doubling his tally of ranking-tournament victories to four. He had started the British Open at Plymouth at odds of 66–1 but wins over Graeme Dott, Ronnie O'Sullivan and Alan McManus took him into the final against Jimmy White, where he disappointed a partisan crowd by defeating the 'People's Champion' by 9–6. His second success came in the Regal Scottish at Aberdeen when he denied Irishman Ken Doherty a hat-trick of ranking titles with a determined 9–7 victory.

Climbing from twelfth to seventh in the world rankings, Ebdon went out of the 2001 World Championship at the quarter-final stage to eventual winner Ronnie O'Sullivan; earlier he had had an emotional outburst after beating Stephen Lee 13–12 in a titanic second-round battle – not the first time that had happened. But he continued to be a model of consistency and reached the final of the LG Cup that season, only to be beaten 9–4 by Stephen Lee.

The following year saw the greatest moment of his career so far. Having beaten Michael Judge (10–4), Joe Perry (13–7) and Anthony Hamilton (13–6) in the early rounds of the 2002 Embassy World Championship, he displayed enormous stamina and mental toughness to come back from 16–14 down to beat Matthew Stevens 17–16 in the semi-final. Then, watched by over 7.5 million viewers, he took a 33–1 shot to win the title, edging out Stephen Hendry 18–17 in the most gripping of finals. Ebdon had led 11–6 but then trailed 14–12 to the Scot. It was neck and neck in the finishing straight but Ebdon clinched victory in the thirty-fifth and final frame – played after midnight – with a decisive break of 59. That victory lifted him to No. 3 in the world rankings and secured a cheque for £260,000, but, as Ebdon pointed out: 'The money is nice but having my name on the trophy alongside all those great names means 100 times more.'

Following his success, Ebdon faced a demanding summer schedule. It included, among other things, giving snooker lessons to the LG Electronics Internet Family in the shop window of Harrods, appearing alongside John McEnroe at Wimbledon, running through York city centre in the Queen's Jubilee Baton Relay as part of the build-up to the Commonwealth Games, and taking part in the BBC's Sports Relief project, just one of countless charity events.

During the early part of the 2002–3 season, Ebdon's form on the table was nothing too special, but in December 2002 he reached the semi-final of the Powerhouse UK Championships before losing 9–3 to Mark Williams.

Although the snooker season can be hectic and involves a great deal of travel, father of four and horse-racing fanatic Peter still finds plenty of time to pursue his hobby and business interest of equine breeding. He owns two brood mares, two yearlings and two foals, and these are based at the Longton stables of Eric Alston. He is also extremely passionate about music and has sung on two pop music singles: the first a remake of David Cassidy's 'I am a Clown' and the second a moody ballad called 'The Fall of Paradise'.

Having played snooker for sixteen years prior to winning the world title, Peter Ebdon described himself as a 'slow learner', but there can't be many who would bet against him repeating the feat in the not-too-distant future.

Terry Griffiths

Born: 16 October 1947, Llanelli, Carmarthenshire

Career highlights
Embassy World Champion 1979

Welsh Amateur Champion 1975
English Amateur Champion 1977, 1978
World Cup Team Winner 1979, 1980
Benson & Hedges Masters Champion 1980
Benson & Hedges Irish Masters Champion 1980, 1981, 1982
Pontin's Professional Champion 1981, 1983
Coral UK Professional Champion 1982
Lada Classic Champion 1982
Pot Black Champion 1984
Welsh Professional Champion 1985

TERRY GRIFFITHS had set his heart on taking part in the 1979 World Amateur Championship in Malta, but Steve Newbury put paid to those plans by beating him in the 1978 Welsh Amateur Championship. Instead Terry turned professional. In his first major professional tournament, the Coral UK Championship, he led Rex Williams 8–2 and needed just one more frame to cause a major upset, but the occasion got the better of him and he lost 9–8. However, in the next tournament, the World Championship at the Crucible, he took the snooker world by storm and, instead of capturing the world amateur title as he had dreamt, he became professional champion of the world.

Griffiths's snooker career developed relatively late, as he was 25 when he appeared in his first Welsh Amateur Championship final in 1972, where he lost to Geoff Thomas. However, between then and 1978 when he turned professional, he enjoyed an outstanding amateur career. In 1975 he gained revenge over Thomas to win his first Welsh title, and in 1977 and 1978 he was twice English amateur champion, scoring easy wins over Grimsby's Sid Hood (13–3) and Bradford's Joe Johnson (13–5). Griffiths was attracting considerable attention by this time. His international career saw him lose just two matches for Wales in the Home International matches, Willie Thorne of England and Scotland's Eddie Sinclair being his only conquerors. As Welsh champion, he took part in the 1976 World Championship in Johannesburg, which was won by his compatriot Doug Mountjoy. Griffiths went out at the quarter-final stage to Jimmy van Rensburg of South Africa just as an all-Welsh final was looking a distinct possibility.

Having turned professional after that 1978 Welsh Championship defeat

by Steve Newbury, Griffiths had to get through the qualifying competition before beating three former finalists on his way to the 1979 World Championship final against Dennis Taylor. First he disposed of Perrie Mans 13–8, then Alex Higgins 13–12 and finally Eddie Charlton 19–17 – the last in a tense and hard-fought semi-final clash that went on until the early hours of the morning. Afterwards, when asked how he felt about his victory, Terry uttered unforgettably in that broad Welsh accent of his, 'I'm in the final now you know'! In that final, he overcame the man who was to win the championship six years later, Dennis Taylor, by 24–16. In doing so, he became the fourth man (following Joe Davis, in the first year of the championships, John Spencer and Alex Higgins) to win the title at his first attempt. He also became the fourth man after John Pulman, John Spencer and Ray Reardon to win the English Amateur title and then the World Professional title.

Later in the year, two narrow defeats prevented him from adding two more important titles to his crown: in the final of the Canadian Open at Toronto he lost by 17–16 to Cliff Thorburn and again by 14–13 to John Virgo in the final of the Coral UK Championships at Preston. However, before the year was out, Terry had added a second world title when, along with Doug Mountjoy and Ray Reardon, he was part of the Welsh team that won the inaugural World Cup. Victory upon victory followed for the likeable Welshman, who admitted that earning a living from snooker was 'money for old rope' compared to the previous jobs he'd had: apprentice blacksmith, postman, miner, bus conductor and insurance salesman.

Griffiths started 1980 as the subject of Eamonn Andrews' famous words 'This is Your Life'; then went on to beat Cliff Thorburn, John Spencer and Alex Higgins to win the Benson & Hedges Masters at the Wembley Conference Centre. He followed this up with the first of three consecutive Benson & Hedges Irish Masters titles, before adding a second world team title as Wales beat Canada in that year's final. His bid to become World Champion for the second year running, however, was foiled by the young London professional Steve Davis, Griffiths losing 13–10, when they met in the second round at the Crucible. Terry swallowed his disappointment and spent the rest of the competition adding his comments on play from the vantage point of the BBC TV commentary box.

Apart from the Irish Masters and Pontin's professional titles, 1981 was a year of near misses and runner-up positions in the Coral UK Championships, Benson & Hedges Masters and World Team Classic. Then, in 1982, Terry won the Lada Classic, beating Steve Davis 9–8 in a great final. Victory was particularly sweet for the Welshman because, until then, Davis had been his bogey-man. Later that year he beat Davis again, 9–5 in the final of the Benson & Hedges Irish Masters. Then, in the final of the Coral UK

Championships, he was involved in one of the game's great matches, finally overcoming Alex Higgins 16–15 at Preston's Guild Hall. After a leaner period, Terry went on to win *Pot Black* in 1984, the Welsh Professional Championship in 1985 and the BCE Belgian Classic in 1986, where he beat Kirk Stevens in the final. In 1987, he opened his own luxury snooker club in his home-town of Llanelli.

The following year saw a revitalized Terry Griffiths, notably at the Crucible where he came close to emulating his performance of nine years earlier. After beating Steve Longworth, Willie Thorne and Neal Foulds, Terry beat Jimmy White in the semi-final before meeting Steve Davis in the final. Having been knocked out of the Embassy World Championships by Davis five times in eight years, Griffiths wryly pointed out: 'It takes the pressure off a bit when Steve's in the other half of the draw.' But in the end there was no avoiding him and Davis made it six wins in nine years, triumphing by 18–11.

Terry Griffiths, who could possibly have been a successful rugby player, having played in the same team as the famous Welsh internationals Phil Bennett and Derek Quinnell, last played at the top in 1997 when he lost 10–9 to Mark Williams in the World Championships at his beloved Crucible. Formerly Director of Coaching of the WPBSA, he is still involved in the sport of snooker, coaching a number of the game's top stars, including current World Champion Mark Williams.

Stephen Hendry

Born: 13 January 1969, Edinburgh, Lothian

Career highlights

Embassy World Champion 1990, 1992, 1993, 1994, 1995, 1996, 1999

Scottish Professional Champion 1986, 1987, 1988
Rothman's Grand Prix Champion 1987, 1990, 1991, 1995
Winfield Masters Champion 1987
British Open Champion 1988, 1991, 1999, 2003
Asian Open Champion 1989, 1990
Benson & Hedges Masters Champion 1989, 1990, 1991, 1992, 1993, 1996
Dubai Duty Free Classic Champion 1989, 1990, 1993
Scottish Masters Champion 1989, 1990, 1995
UK Champion 1989, 1990, 1994, 1995, 1996
Regal Welsh Champion 1992, 1997, 2003
European Open Champion 1993, 1994, 2001
Regal Scottish Champion 1997, 1999
Thailand Masters Champion 1998

WHEN IT COMES to a debate on the greatest snooker player of all time, there can, in my opinion, be only one conclusion: Stephen Hendry. Just as Ray Reardon ruled snooker in the 1970s and Steve Davis dominated the 1980s, so Stephen Hendry was emphatically the player of the 1990s. No. 1 in the world-ranking list for eight successive seasons, he has compiled more than 600 century breaks and amassed over £7 million in his eighteen-year career. The winner of thirty-four ranking events, Hendry has rewritten the record books.

Since first appearing on *Junior Pot Black* as a tiny 14-year-old, barely able to see over the table, the burden of 'infant prodigy' has inevitably been thrust upon his slender shoulders. When he won the Scottish Under-16 title the same year, the weight of those expectations increased, but this did not prevent him becoming the youngest Scottish amateur champion the following season.

On turning professional, he captured the 1986 Scottish professional title when still only 17 and the following year he not only retained the title but also won the *Winfield Masters* in Australia. Then, at 18, he became the youngest winner of a ranking tournament, beating Dennis Taylor 10–7 to win the Rothman's Grand Prix. A further win that season in the MIM Britannia British Open helped elevate him from No. 23 to No. 4 in the world rankings. Although he was without a ranking win in 1988–9, he managed to lift some titles, notably the Benson & Hedges Masters at Wembley, where he beat John Parrott.

On 29 April 1990, he became, at 21 years 106 days, the youngest ever winner of the World Championship when he beat Jimmy White 18–12. The

'Whirlwind' was subsequently on the receiving end for three successive finals, the first in 1992, when Hendry, having lost 13–11 to Steve James in the quarter-finals the previous year, regained his title, beating White 18–14. White had led 14–8 and at 14–9 had been 52 points ahead in the last frame of the penultimate session. Hendry had a chance to clear but had to play a very awkward brown at dead weight from almost tight on the cushion to leave position on the yellow. Had he failed, White would almost certainly have led 15–9 going into the final session. In fact, Hendry stroked the brown in and cleared up to trail by only four frames instead of six, after which he went on to secure victory without White winning another frame. In the 1993 World Championship, Hendry was in a class of his own, winning the title with a frame tally of 70–25 and beating Jimmy White 18–5 with a session of the final to spare. The following year Hendry sustained a hairline fracture just below his elbow in a bathroom fall early in the World Championship. It seemed inconceivable that he could retain the title. He was in great pain and had to rest the arm in a sling between matches, but somehow he reached the final. On the deciding thirty-fifth frame, White seemed to have it in the bag, being in play with enough open reds to clinch the title, but, in a moment he will remember as long as he lives, he missed the black from its spot. Hendry rose from his chair to make an ice-cool 58 for frame, match and championship.

In the 1995 World Championship, Hendry was to beat White again, this time in the semi-finals – a match in which he was to record his second maximum break, his first having come in the European League. He went on to record a comfortable 18–9 win over Nigel Bond in the final. On 25 November of the same year, in the UK Championship, Hendry became the first player to make more than two tournament 147s. Not content with that, he made his fourth maximum on 5 January 1997 in the final of the Liverpool Victoria Charity Challenge when, after losing six successive frames against Ronnie O'Sullivan, he completed a 9–8 victory. Then, on 23 May 1998 in the Dr Marten's Premier League, he completed an incredible fifth maximum.

Hendry's sixth world title arrived through an 18–12 victory over Peter Ebdon in the 1996 final. Ebdon, mentally jaded by three epic wins over Steve Davis, Jimmy White and Ronnie O'Sullivan, was no match for the Scot, who, despite not being in vintage form, deservedly triumphed. Hendry's run of twenty-nine consecutive victories at the Crucible was ended by Ken Doherty in the 1997 World Championship final, and he then lost 10–4 to Jimmy White in the first round of the next year's competition. Nevertheless Hendry remained supremely confident that a record seventh world crown would ultimately be his. Sure enough, in 1999 he beat Mark Williams 18–11 to secure that coveted seventh title, an achievement that prompted Hendry to say: 'Without doubt, this is worth more than the other six titles put together. It was the one last ambition I had in snooker and I've proved I can do it.'

Hendry's hopes of an eighth world crown were dashed by little-known Stuart Bingham in the first round of the 2000 tournament, and he was outplayed by Matthew Stevens in the quarter-finals the following year, but the Scot ended the most barren spell of his illustrious professional career by winning the European Open for a third time in December 2001. He went on to reach his ninth World Championship final in 2002 but went down 18–17 to Peter Ebdon in a gripping match. The Scot gave a brutally honest assessment of his performance, saying: 'I never thought I would see the day when I bottled the chance to win the World Championship. I had two great chances in the last frame and I can't believe the way I collapsed. I am absolutely gutted and I have no one to blame but myself.'

Early in 2003 he proved that his best years are not yet behind him, when he won the Regal Welsh trophy for a record third time, knocking in four centuries in the final to beat World Champion Mark Williams 9–5, in a performance reminiscent of his heyday. His form continued to impress, and he beat Ronnie O'Sullivan to win the 2003 British Open Championship.

Widely regarded by his fellow professionals as the greatest player ever to pick up a cue, he was voted the World Professional Billiards and Snooker Association's Player of the Year in 1990, 1991, 1992, 1993, 1995, 1996 and 1997. He was awarded an MBE by the Queen in 1994.

Alex Higgins

Born: 18 March 1949, Belfast, Northern Ireland

Career highlights
Embassy World Champion 1972, 1982

All Ireland Amateur Champion 1968
Northern Ireland Amateur Champion 1968
Canadian Open Champion 1975, 1977
Pontin's Open Champion 1977
Benson & Hedges Masters Champion 1978, 1981
Tolly Cobbold Classic Champion 1979, 1980
British Gold Cup Champion 1980
Coral UK Professional Champion 1983
Irish Professional Champion 1983
World Doubles Champion 1984
World Cup Team Winner 1985

ALEX HIGGINS, the mercurial Irishman who changed the face of snooker after winning the World Championship in 1972, could do no wrong in the eyes of his legion of admirers. Domestic dramas, public rows and punch-ups, they seemed never ending, but Higgins took them all in his stride and carried on with what he did best. He remained a prime attraction on the circuit, tournament sponsors always being grateful when the 'Hurricane' blew into town looking for action on the green baize.

If he had had his own way and sufficient dedication, Alex Higgins would probably have been a professional jockey instead of a snooker player. Though he had played snooker since the age of 11 at the Jampot Club, not far from his council house home in Belfast where he lived with his three sisters, he left home at 14 to join the Eddie Reavey racing stable. At that time he weighed just over 7 stone, but in the two and a half years he was with Reavey his weight shot up to 11 stone and he left without enjoying a competitive ride. He moved to London and worked in a paper-mill for a while and it was during this time that he took up snooker again in the Soho billiard halls. Returning to Ireland, he started playing in the Belfast and District Snooker League for the City YMCA Club captained by George Connell, and it was on the table at Connell's home in 1965 that Higgins compiled his first century break. Three years later, he won both the All Ireland and Northern Ireland amateur titles.

Higgins turned professional in 1971 and promptly won the Irish Championship from Jack Rea. The brash youngster, already branded a hell-raiser by some, had been shouting from the rooftops in Muhammad Ali fashion: 'I am the greatest. I will be the new world champion!' Those who saw

Higgins in action throughout the 1972 World Championship (at that time spread over several months) could hardly deny he was the most exciting talent yet to emerge on the snooker scene. However, he had flirted with danger against Rex Williams in the semi-finals, scraping through 31–30 after coming within a blue ball of defeat. His opponent in the final was John Spencer, who had won the World Championship in 1969 and regained it in 1971, but Higgins, already dubbed the 'Hurricane' because of the speed with which he dispatched balls from all over the table, was the firm favourite to take the title.

The first session at the Selly Park British Legion in Birmingham ended all square at six frames apiece, but by the end of the second day Spencer had taken a 13–11 lead. On day three, Higgins slipped three frames behind, 17–14, only to draw level again at 18–18 by the end of the evening. The players were all square once again after the first six frames of day four, but then Higgins suddenly cut loose to take a 27–21 lead. The Irishman almost brought the roof down with some spectacular play, but then nerves took a hold and Spencer clawed his way back into the game, the day ending with Alex just 32–28 in front. As the final day unfolded, errors crept in on both sides, and, with the

Alex Higgins with his wife, Lynn, holding aloft the World Championship trophy in 1982.

score at 33–32 in Higgins's favour, the world champion was still in with a chance of retaining his crown. But Higgins would not be denied, taking the next four frames to clinch a memorable 37–32 victory, and to become at the age of 22 the youngest ever world champion until Hendry's triumph in 1990.

For all his brilliance, the flamboyant Ulsterman was to wait another decade before winning snooker's richest prize a second time. He did so in 1982, beating Ray Reardon 18–15 amid scenes of tears and laughter, after which he emotionally declared: 'Now I can die happy'. He followed up this success with a spectacular 16–15 win against Steve Davis in the 1983 Coral UK final, coming back from 7–0 down in a performance that must surely be ranked as snooker's second greatest comeback, topped only by Dennis Taylor's famous black-ball world title victory over Davis eighteen months later.

There was, of course, another side to Alex Higgins. Highly strung and fuelled by nervous energy, he was never far away from controversy, which sometimes cost him dear. For example, his first world title earned him just £480, a fraction of the £12,000 he was fined for, among other offences, head-butting tournament director Paul Hatherall during the 1986 Tennents UK Open at Preston, an incident that also earned him a five-tournament ban. On another occasion, the 1986 Mercantile Credit Classic at Warrington, he turned up sporting a black eye and claiming to have fallen off a horse. The press and public laughed it off, but a day later the Irishman came clean and confessed that he'd actually been hit by a fellow professional during a private argument. Such incidents, however, merely added to the legend of the tempestuous but engaging Irishman, his colourful play on the table matched by an equally colourful lifestyle off it! When his private life, including the break-up of his six-year marriage to wife Lynn, was laid bare to the public in the pages of the popular press, it inspired as much sympathy as criticism, and when, in October 1988, he found a glimmer of his best form to battle his way through to the Rothman's final, the crowd loved him all the more. That he lost to Steve Davis mattered little. Typically, Alex rescued the after-match banquet following the departure of the world champion by playing an exhibition game in 'Hurricane' style after a dispute between the sponsors and the Matchroom group.

Alex Higgins was a supreme entertainer. He may not have performed trick shots like Steve Davis, told jokes like Dennis Taylor, or done impressions like John Virgo, but fans still poured in to watch the 'People's Champion'. Higgins remained the game's most popular player many years after his decline as a major force in world snooker. He still plays a few exhibition matches, but poor health has prevented him from taking part in competitive action for some time. Some will remember him as volatile and unpredictable, but for his many fans Alex Higgins on his day was, quite simply, the greatest snooker player in the world.

John Higgins

Born: 18 May 1975, Wishaw, North Lanarkshire

Career highlights
Embassy World Champion 1998

Rothman's Grand Prix Champion 1994, 1999
British Open Champion 1995, 1998, 2001
German Open Champion 1995, 1997
International Champion 1995, 1996
World Cup Team Winner 1996
European Open Champion 1997
Liverpool Victoria UK Champion 1998, 2000
Regal China International Champion 1999
Regal Welsh Champion 2000
Coalite Nations Cup Winner 2001
Regal Scottish Champion 2001

JOHN HIGGINS, the 'Wizard of Wishaw', enjoyed his greatest moment in snooker at the Crucible in 1998, beating Ken Doherty 18–12 to win the world title. The victory made Higgins the third Scottish winner of snooker's blue riband event and gave him the world No. 1 spot, which he held for two seasons.

Higgins's introduction to World Championship snooker was a quiet affair, ending with an early exit during pre-qualifying in 1993 following a 5–2 defeat to Michael Gold. A year later he was beaten in a qualifying round again, as Leigh Robinson won by 10 frames to 9. However, 1994 saw him claim his first ranking event – the Rothman's Grand Prix – beating Dave Harold 9–6 in the final, and he captured two more titles that season, the International Open and Castella Classic British Open.

Higgins first played in the World Championship at the Crucible in 1995 but was well beaten 10–3 by compatriot Alan McManus in the first round. He did little to endear himself to the Crucible devotees when he declared after his exit: 'This place did nothing for me.' By his own admission, he struggled during the following season, to produce the level of performance needed. The quest for perfection in his cue, which spent more time at the cue doctors than it did in its case, seemed to have an adverse effect on his self-belief. Nevertheless he managed to win one tournament – the 1997 European Open in Malta – overcoming John Parrott 9–5 in the final.

In 1996 John Higgins missed the chance to become the youngest ever world champion. Heading for victory in his quarter-final match against Ronnie O'Sullivan, he was forced, in the twenty-fourth frame, to use the rest to complete a match-winning clearance of 65, but he missed the pink into

the top pocket. O'Sullivan, 10–5 behind overnight, took the frame on the black before going on to win the match 13–12.

The following season, having won two world-ranking tournaments – the German Open in 1997 and the 1998 British Open – Higgins, in order to become the world No. 1, needed both to win the Embassy title and to see Stephen Hendry go out in the first round. Hendry duly lost 10–4 to Jimmy White, and, after a scare in his first-round match against Jason Ferguson, Higgins scraped home 10–8. He then found himself 6–2 down to Anthony Hamilton in round two before running out the winner at 13–9. His quarter-final match with John Parrott was a classic, both men playing some fantastic snooker, but Higgins finally triumphed 13–11. In the semi-final against Ronnie O'Sullivan, having been held to 4–4 in the early stages, he pulled away to win rather easily 17–9, going on in the final to defeat the previous year's world champion, Ken Doherty, 18–12, having led throughout the match. During the course of that championship, Higgins had made a record fourteen century breaks. Later that season, he won the UK Championship, thus becoming only the fourth man behind Stephen Hendry, Steve Davis and John Parrott to achieve the World and UK double. He followed this up with victory in the Liverpool Victoria Charity Challenge.

In 1999, as well as winning the Regal China International title and the

Rothman's Grand Prix, Higgins reached the semi-finals of the World Championship, where he lost 17–10 to Mark Williams. The Welshman once again put paid to Higgins's hopes of regaining his title the following year, winning 17–15 after Higgins had been 15–11 ahead. For Higgins, this was surely the lowest point of his career, but later that year he captured his second UK title when he beat David Gray (9–6), Peter Ebdon (9–4), Drew Henry (9–6) and Stephen Hendry (9–4) before gaining revenge over Mark Williams in the final with a 10–4 victory. His return to form was aided by official world snooker coach Richy McDonald, who was there to support him throughout that tournament, staged at the Bournemouth International Centre. Higgins had known McDonald since his amateur days, both of them practising at the same club, The Masters, at Dennistoun, Glasgow. In 2000, against Northern Ireland's Dennis Taylor during the Nations Cup, Higgins compiled his first maximum break in professional competition, following this up in January 2001 by helping Scotland lift the trophy for the first time.

Later that year, after beating Graeme Dott (10–4), Chris Small (13–8), Ken Doherty (13–6) and Matthew Stevens (17–15), Higgins reached his second World Championship final, where his opponent was Ronnie O'Sullivan. 'You have to win the World Championship two or three times before you can be classed as a true great of the game,' said Higgins, but after losing the first session 6–2 he was always playing catch-up. Try as he might, he could never quite close the gap, finally going down 18–14. He soon bounced back, however, beating Mark Williams 7–4 at the Brighton Centre to win the Champions Cup for the first time. In his next outing he won his first title on home soil, beating Ronnie O'Sullivan 9–6 in the final of the Regal Scottish Masters at Glasgow's Thistle Hotel and, in so doing, halting a five-match losing streak against the 'Rocket'. He then completed a hat-trick by beating fellow Scot Graeme Dott 9–6 in the final of the British Open at Newcastle's Telewest Arena. This made John Higgins the first player to win the opening three tournaments of a campaign and he finished the season at the top of the money list with £486,850.

A recent decline in form coincided with the birth of his first child, as Higgins sacrificed time on the practice table to get to know his son Pierce. Quarter-final defeats in the 2002 and 2003 World Championships to Matthew Stevens (13–7) and Ken Doherty (13–8) respectively have seen Higgins drop a place in the rankings for three successive years – to No. 4 in 2003 – but the popular Scot, who stands third on the all-time winners list behind Stephen Hendry and Steve Davis, hopes to reverse that trend soon. Indeed, in November 2003, he created history by becoming the first player ever to record a maximum 147 break in two successive tournaments.

Joe Johnson

Born: 29 July 1952, Bradford, West Yorkshire

Career highlights
Embassy World Champion 1986

National Under-19 Snooker Champion 1971
Scottish Masters Champion 1987

LESS THAN a week before the first anniversary of the appalling Valley Parade fire tragedy, Bradford-born Joe Johnson warmed the hearts of West Yorkshire people by lifting the world crown. It was scant consolation, of course, for those who had lost loved ones in the tragedy, but those who knew Joe knew that his win was as much for the people of Bradford as for himself.

Joe Johnson was an excellent snooker player long before he stunned Steve Davis and won the world title. He preceded Tony Knowles as National Under-19 Snooker Champion in 1971, and in 1978 was runner-up to Terry Griffiths in the English Amateur Championship. That performance earned him the right to compete in the World Amateur Championship that year in Malta, where he lost to Cliff Wilson, after reaching the final. Johnson represented England on ten occasions in the Home International Championships – Griffiths being one of only two men to beat him. He was also for many years the holder of the world record break by an amateur, after compiling a 140 at the Middlesbrough TUC in 1978. That achievement was covered by Tyne-Tees television, but in fact, Joe had something of a mental block about playing in front of TV cameras. He maintained that the lights put him off, and his victory in the Professional Players' Tournament at Bristol's Redwood Lodge in 1983, which saw him beat such eminent players as Tony Meo, Jimmy White, Eddie Charlton and Cliff Thorburn en route to his first major final, seemed to confirm that claim – it was not a televised event! In that final, against the in-form Tony Knowles, Johnson came back from 6–1 down before finally losing 9–8 but not until he had compiled a championship-best break of 135. Two years later, he reached the semi-final of the 1985 Mercantile Credit Classic before losing 9–2 to Cliff Thorburn – a performance that helped to lift Joe into the top sixteen for the first time.

At the end of the 1985–6 season, after only twice reaching the Crucible stage of the World Championships, Johnson secured that memorable title victory that was to make him the darling of the Sheffield fans. Despite developing a nasty back ulcer shortly before the tournament began, Joe beat Geordie Dave Martin 10–3 in his opening match. In the next round he faced Mike Hallett, who had pulled off the shock of the previous round by toppling defending champion Dennis Taylor. A 13–6 victory took Johnson to the

quarter-finals, where his opponent was Terry Griffiths. The Welshman started out favourite, but Joe won the first three frames and later in the day led 6–3. However, Terry Griffiths was one of the game's great battlers and he pulled back to be down just 9–7 overnight. Indeed, Griffiths could have counted himself unfortunate not to be on level terms, for in the last frame of that session Johnson had luckily covered the final red with the black after it had been left over a baulk pocket. The following morning Johnson missed a straightforward black, allowing Griffiths to take the first frame. Terry won the next as well to level the scores at 9–9 and then shattered Joe by winning three frames on the trot to take a 12–9 lead. However, in the next frame, Griffiths made an error, allowing Johnson to make a break of 102 and so recapture his confidence. From that point on, Johnson played some phenomenal snooker – a frame-winning break of 43 came next followed by a spectacular 110 to draw level. In the deciding frame, Johnson ran in a swift 54 before completing the match with a break of 33 to clinch his semi-final place 13–12. What a session – five in a row from Griffiths and then four in just fifty-two minutes from the man who, until a week earlier, had never tasted victory at the Crucible! It was a truly classic encounter. Johnson then roared past Tony Knowles 16–8 in the semi-finals before dismantling the overwhelming favourite, Steve Davis, 18–12 in the final itself. The 150–1 outsider had claimed his place in snooker history in the most emphatic manner, celebrating his success afterwards with a pint of lager with his friends at the Morley Snooker Centre near Bradford.

Ironically, Joe's success looked for a time like being his downfall. Eager to share his glory with the people who had helped and supported him over the years, he undertook dozens of exhibitions and attended numerous charity functions. As a result his game began to fall apart, and by the time the World Championship came round again Joe was not even considered a contender for the title. After a nervy 10–9 win over Eugene Hughes in the first round and a slightly easier victory over Murdo McLeod in the next, Johnson found himself up against Stephen Hendry. The Yorkshireman led 8–1 and Hendry came back at him, but Joe clung on for a terrific 13–12 win. In the semi-final Johnson beat Neal Foulds 16–9 and suddenly found himself in the Crucible's first ever repeat final. Sadly for Joe it was not a repeat result in his favour, as Davis won 18–14. The following year, the up-and-coming Steve James ended Johnson's ambition of a hat-trick of final appearances, but Joe still managed to maintain his position among the elite top sixteen of the game.

Success has never gone to Johnson's head – he remembers his days as a trainee mechanic and then a pipe-layer too well for that. Still playing on the main tour as well as being a board member of World Snooker, he counts himself fortunate to get paid for playing the game he loves.

Tony Knowles

Born: 13 June 1955, Bolton, Lancashire

Career highlights
National Under-19 Snooker Champion 1972, 1974
Jameson International Champion 1982
Professional Players' Tournament Champion 1983
World Cup Team Winner 1983
Winfield Masters Champion 1984

TONY KNOWLES had the world at his fingertips in 1982 when he crushed Steve Davis 10–1 to end his reign as World Champion, and when Tony went on to clinch the Jameson International title a few months later, as the new season unfolded, it seemed nothing could stop him stepping into Davis's shoes.

Tony, who comes from the author's home town of Bolton, started playing snooker at the age of 9. His father was steward at the Tonge Moor Conservative Club where the young Tony managed to practise on the club's full-sized table. A proficient player by the age of 16, he had the thrill then of meeting and playing his idol, Alex Higgins, in occasional exhibition matches. He went on to Art College, where he qualified as a graphic artist, but on leaving at the age of 18 he decided to embark on a full-time snooker career. The late Jim Worsley – the man instrumental in bringing Alex Higgins to England in the 1970s – took an interest in Knowles's early progress, and saw him win the national Under-19 Championship at his first attempt, beating Matt Gibson of Glasgow in the 1972 final. On the morning of that final, Tony compiled the first century break of his career. Two years later, he won the title for a second time, beating Paul Smith of Hitchen in the final. Knowles represented England in the Home International Championships in 1978 and 1979, playing a total of nine matches and winning them all. His five wins in 1979 earned him the 'Player of the Series' award. That year also saw his first individual success, for he won three important amateur tournaments, including a £1,000 first prize in the Pontin's autumn festival.

Knowles turned professional at the beginning of 1980 but was too late to qualify for that year's World Championship. After a patient year of waiting and exhibition matches, he entered his first World Championship in 1981 but was beaten 10–8 in the first round by Graham Miles. Better was to follow at the Coral UK Professional Championship at Preston, his victories there including a 9–6 defeat of Doug Mountjoy before he went down 9–5 against Terry Griffiths in the quarter-finals. The following year, however, saw Knowles create one of the biggest upsets in snooker history when he secured that

stunning victory over defending champion Steve Davis in the 1982 World Championship. The snooker world watched astounded as Knowles raced into a 4–0 lead before Davis won a single frame and was even more amazed when he ended the evening session 8–1 in front. Any talk of a Davis comeback the next day was soon dispelled as Knowles won the first two frames of the opening session to record a memorable 10–1 victory. Knowles then beat Graham Miles before losing narrowly to Australian Eddie Charlton in the quarter-finals. Later that year he won his first major professional title, the Jameson International, beating Dennis Taylor in the final. His second success came the following year when he beat Joe Johnson in the final of the Professional Players' Tournament by 9–8 at Redwood Lodge in Bristol. Then, in the 1983 World Championship, Knowles reached the semi-finals, only, when in a very strong position, to miss a simple pink and allow Cliff Thorburn to save the frame and go through at his expense.

The next year was to bring controversy as a colourful account of Knowles's private life appeared in a national newspaper just before the 1984 World Championship. It hardly enhanced his reputation as a snooker player. The

Tony Knowles at the table. His opponent is Terry Griffiths.

WPBSA, furious that television's fastest-growing sport had, in its eyes, been cheapened, fined him a record £5,000. From world No. 2 Tony slipped down the rankings yet managed to earn enough points in ensuing seasons to retain a top ten position, confounding critics by securing valuable ranking points with his fast, fluent potting style. Then a second bombshell dropped, when a former girlfriend joined the list of those ready to sell their secrets. Vigorously denying the claims made, Knowles sensibly maintained a discreet profile for the next twelve months.

Gradually, through sheer hard work, Knowles regained the cutting edge that his game had been lacking. Though it was not enough to get back on the title-winning trail, it was good enough to beat all but the best. A curious incident that aided his rehabilitation occurred in the 1988 Benson & Hedges Masters at Wembley when his stablemate Alex Higgins picked an argument during their match. Knowles had been in full control, holding a 3–1 lead, when the volatile Irishman complained to the referee that Tony was putting him off by standing in his line of vision, a claim dismissed by Knowles as sheer gamesmanship. When the row spilled over into the interval, the Wembley tournament director was called in to act as peacemaker, but Knowles's game subsequently fell apart and he went on to lose 5–4. Inwardly he was seething, but wisely confined his remarks to the simple: 'You all saw what happened out there.' He was seen by most as the aggrieved party, and his stock went up considerably, both inside the game and with the fans.

A fitness fanatic and all-round sportsman, Knowles actively participated in swimming, cycling, squash, golf and tennis, and appeared on the BBC Television's *Superstars* programme. Regarded as snooker's top pin-up, the likeable Lancastrian did exceptionally well from the sport. As well as a snooker centre in the middle of Horwich, on the outskirts of his native Bolton, he owns several properties, including a beautifully appointed house on the banks of Lake Windermere, where he indulges his passion for the great outdoors and water-skiing.

Doug Mountjoy

Born: 8 June 1942, Tir-y-Berth, Glamorgan

Career highlights

Welsh Amateur Champion 1968, 1976
National Breaks Champion 1970
Pontin's Open Champion 1974, 1976
World Amateur Champion 1976
Benson & Hedges Masters Champion 1977
Pot Black Champion 1978
UK Professional Champion 1978, 1988
Benson & Hedges Irish Masters Champion 1979
Pontin's Professional Champion 1979, 1983
World Cup Team Winner 1979, 1980
Champion of Champions 1980
Welsh Professional Champion 1980, 1982, 1984
Mercantile Credit Classic Champion 1989

BORN IN Tir-y-Berth in the Rhymney Valley, Doug Mountjoy became Junior Valley Champion at the age of 15 and, by the time he joined his father down the mine a year later, he was one of the best players in South Wales. However, career prospects in snooker during the 1960s were limited, there being only three or four professionals in the game, so Doug at that time did not even entertain the idea of playing snooker as a trade. It was to take a string of successes as an amateur to make him change his mind. Runner-up in the 1966 Welsh Amateur Championship, he went on to win the title in 1968 and again in 1976, during which period, as well as twice winning the Pontin's Open, he also represented Wales in international tournaments, winning against both John Virgo (England) and Patsy Fagan (Ireland). In October 1976 he took part in the World Amateur Snooker Championships at the President Hotel in Johannesburg. Twenty-four players competed and Doug, playing in Group One, won all his seven games to reach the final, where his unfortunate opponent, Paul Mifsud of Malta, won just one frame out of twelve!

Subsequently invited to play in *Pot Black*, he decided it was time to turn professional after all. His first appearance in 1977 saw him reach the final, but he was well beaten by Perrie Mans. Later that year, having beaten John Pulman, Fred Davis and Alex Higgins, he met Ray Reardon in the final of the Benson & Hedges Masters at the London Theatre, Drury Lane. Mountjoy won 7–6 to claim his first major title. In 1978 he reached the final of *Pot Black* for the second year running. Playing against Graham Miles, he won two of the three frames, scoring the highest break of 101, to earn the title of *Pot Black*

Champion 1978. The following year he competed in the Coral UK Professional Championships at Preston's Guild Hall, a tournament that saw him beat David Taylor in the final to achieve yet another important snooker honour. The new UK champion then played in his third series of *Pot Black* and reached the final for the third year in succession. Though Ray Reardon beat him 2–1, Mountjoy again won the highest break prize and the Joe Davis trophy with a score of 82. Doug then took his revenge on Reardon, defeating him in the final of the Benson & Hedges Masters in Ireland. Later that year he returned to the scene of some of his amateur triumphs – the Pontin's Snooker Festival at Prestatyn – on this occasion playing against his professional colleagues, beating Graham Miles in the final. Then, as 1979 drew to a close, he formed part of the Welsh trio, along with Terry Griffiths and Ray Reardon, that beat England in the State Express World Cup final.

The following year saw mixed fortunes for Mountjoy. There was disappointment for him in the World Championship but, as well as winning the Woodpecker Welsh Professional Championship held in Ebbw Vale, beating

Ray Reardon in the final, he won the title 'Champion of Champions' after a round-robin contest in which he defeated John Virgo 10–8 in the final. Then with the same partners as the previous year, he was part of the Welsh side that retained the State Express World Championship at the Crucible. Shortly afterwards he suffered an attack of Bell's palsy, which paralysed one side of his face and affected the blinking function of one eyelid. This inevitably affected his performances for some time but the 1983 World Championship saw an emphatic return to form, his break of 145 against Ray Reardon in the semi-final earning him £1,200 for the highest break in the tournament plus £5,000 for the second highest break in the history of the championship. Seeded 14, he had fought his way to the semi-final with victories over Willie Thorne, Eddie Charlton and Dennis Taylor and when he also saw off Ray Reardon he was through to the final. He lost 18–12 to Steve Davis, but at least had the consolation of an additional £10,000 received as the runner-up.

There subsequently followed more than half a decade in the doldrums

during which Mountjoy slipped out of the top sixteen. In despair, he turned
to the coaching guru Frank Callan, who, well aware of Mountjoy's natural
ability, set about painstakingly refashioning the Welshman's game to put his
once-illustrious pupil back on the title trail. Both, Callan and Mountjoy
expected it would take some time – perhaps even a year or two – before all
the hard work paid off, so to reach the final of the 1988 Tennents UK Open a
few months later must have been beyond his wildest dreams. Doug's
opponent in the final was the up-and-coming Stephen Hendry. The scores
were level at 7–7 at the end of the first day but then Mountjoy collected the
first two frames of the following afternoon and eased himself into the form of
his life. He went into the interval having scored 222 points without reply
and, more significantly, with a lead of 11–7. The odds swung dramatically in
the Welshman's favour as he won the next frame and then followed up with
two consecutive centuries – a 131 and a 106. There was more to come as
Doug compiled a 124, a third consecutive 100 break for a record-breaking
frame for victory. Hendry came back strongly to win the next five frames, but,
when the young Scotsman made a mistake in the next frame, Doug was
sufficiently composed to win the title and a place in snooker folklore. Amid
scenes that evoked Dennis Taylor's unforgettable win over Steve Davis in the
1985 World Championship, the tears and tributes poured out for both Doug
and Frank Callan. Doug neatly summed up the achievement when the game
was over: 'Reaching the final was like swimming the Channel,' he said 'but
winning it is like swimming the Atlantic!' To add to that success, Mountjoy
won the next ranking event, the Mercantile Credit Classic, beating his former
practice partner Wayne Jones in the final.

One of four members of the tiny Abertysswg club to have won the Welsh
amateur title – Alwyn Lloyd, Des May and Wayne Jones being the others –
Mountjoy subsequently left his home near Ebbw Vale to move across the
Welsh border and take over the Temple Bar Inn at Ewyas Harold in
Herefordshire.

Ronnie O'Sullivan

Born: 5 December 1975, Chigwell, London

Career highlights
Embassy World Champion 2001

UK Champion 1993, 1997, 2001
British Open Champion 1994
Asian Classic Champion 1996
German Open Champion 1996
Regal Scottish Champion 1998, 2000, 2002
China Open Champion 1999, 2000
Benson & Hedges Irish Masters Champion 2003
European Open Champion 2003
Regal Masters Champion 2003

ANY FEARS that Ronnie O'Sullivan had of succeeding Jimmy White as 'the greatest player never to win the world title' were dispelled during the 2001 World Championships, the 'Rocket' proving that he had the stamina and concentration necessary to last the seventeen-day marathon at the Crucible.

O'Sullivan started playing the game on a six-foot table when he was 8, graduating to a full-size table a year later. His father took him down to Brooksby's in Hackney, and the young O'Sullivan practised with a top amateur by the name of Marcus Owen. It was clear from an early age that Ronnie O'Sullivan, who made his first century break at the age of 10, had star quality. At the age of 15 years and 97 days he became the youngest player to compile a recognized maximum break outside professional competition during the England Amateur Championship, and at 16 years 9 months he was the youngest player to qualify for the televised stages of the World Championship.

In 1992 O'Sullivan turned professional, winning seventy-five out of seventy-seven matches in qualifying for ranking events and making a record thirty centuries in his debut season. A year later, at 17 years 11 months, he became the youngest player to win a ranking title when he captured the UK Championship, beating Stephen Hendry 10–6 in the final. In 1994 he won the British Open and was named the WPBSA's Player of the Year. In doing so, he amassed £285,101 in prize money, the largest amount a teenager has earned in a single season.

Displaying an extraordinary ability to knock in high breaks, both right- and left-handed, O'Sullivan won the Masters the following year, beating John Higgins in the final. Then, in 1996, he was involved in an epic match with Peter Ebdon in the World Championship semi-finals. At one point O'Sullivan was 10–5 down, but seven frames later the scores were level at 11–11.

Unfortunately for Ronnie, Ebdon pulled away to win 16–14. Such was Ebdon's admiration for the player he had just beaten that he put an arm round him afterwards and said 'You're a genius.'

In the 1997 World Championship O'Sullivan fired in the quickest 147 on record, his maximum taking just 5 minutes 20 seconds during a 10–6 first-round win over Mick Price, but his dream of becoming world champion was then shattered 13–12 by Darren Morgan in round two. The 147, however, was worth £165,000 in total (a £147,000 bonus plus £18,000 for the highest break) – or £515.62 per second! It smashed the previous best of 7 minutes 9 seconds established by James Wattana against Tony Drago in the 1992 British Open at Derby. Manoeuvring the cue ball around the table with effortless assurance, O'Sullivan's play was flawless. His cue-ball control was so precise that he was not required to pot a difficult ball throughout. After sinking the opening red from distance and simultaneously developing the black, 'Rocket' Ronnie chipped away at the pack of reds at every opportunity. The best shot of the break was the fifteenth black, pocketed by O'Sullivan into a top corner while stunning the white off two cushions into perfect position for the yellow. Later that season, Ronnie won the UK Championship, beating Stephen Hendry 10–6 in the final, and the Regal Scottish with a 9–5 victory over John Higgins. A year later, however, he failed to defend his UK title, withdrawing from the tournament suffering from nervous exhaustion.

During the course of the 1998–9 season, O'Sullivan recorded another televised 147. It came in his Regal Welsh quarter-final in Cardiff against Thailand's James Wattana and lasted 6 minutes 51 seconds – a leisurely stroll compared to his incredible Crucible effort. The following season he made two more maximums, in the Grand Prix and the Regal Scottish. He was a beaten semi-finalist, however, in the World Championships of 1998 (by John Higgins) and 1999 (by Stephen Hendry), and some questioned O'Sullivan's commitment and desire when he surprisingly lost 10–9 to David Gray in 2000. In fact, there was even talk of retirement! Thankfully, though, it all came right during the 2000–1 season – the most successful of Ronnie's career to date – as he won six titles: the Champions' Cup, Regal Masters, China Open, Citywest Irish Masters, Sportingbet.co.uk Premier League and, of course, the World Championship. O'Sullivan was on cruise control for much of the latter, dispatching Andy Hicks (10–2), Dave Harold (13–6), Peter Ebdon (13–6) and Joe Swail (17–11) to reach his first world final. There, after building a first-session lead of 6–2 over Scotland's John Higgins, he went on to win 18–14 to become the first Englishman to lift the trophy since John Parrott in 1991. In doing so, he not only boosted his bank balance with a cheque for £3,250,000 but secured second place in the world rankings ahead of Higgins. More important still, he finally fulfilled the precocious talent he had shown as a teenager. As he said: 'It has taken me a little longer than people were expecting. I didn't want the tag of being the best player never to win the world title.'

The following season O'Sullivan won his third UK title in nine years, beating Ken Doherty 10–1 in the 2001 final at York. His toughest match was the quarter-final, Peter Ebdon having surged into a 6–1 lead and then going 8–4 up in the evening session, but with a characteristic burst of brilliance – knocking in four breaks of over 70 – the 'Rocket' subsequently reeled off five frames to clinch an unlikely 9–8 victory. Later in the season he made a strong defence of his world title but succumbed to Stephen Hendry in the semi-final. The two snooker giants were locked at 12–12 before the Scot pulled away to win in the final session 17–13.

In 2002–3 O'Sullivan won the Regal Masters, beating John Higgins in the final 9–4, then added the European Open title in March, beating Stephen Hendry 9–6, and won the Irish Masters, beating John Higgins 10–9 in a dramatic final frame shoot-out in which O'Sullivan won with a 128 total clearance. He subsequently tumbled out of the World Championship, losing his first-round match against Marco Fu, but not before he had brought the house down at the Crucible with a brilliant 147 maximum break, taking just 6 minutes 30 seconds to earn himself £169,000. At the time of writing he has compiled six maximums, including the five fastest of all time.

Some may feel that O'Sullivan has not had quite the impact on snooker that his talent promised, but this is to overlook the emergence of other outstanding players on the circuit such as Mark Williams and John Higgins as well as the up-and-coming Paul Hunter. Ken Doherty and Peter Ebdon have also maintained consistently high levels of performance in what is, by some margin, the most competitive era in snooker history. Showing much courage in bouncing back from a string of recent personal problems, Ronnie is full of fresh enthusiasm and looking forward to a bright future.

John Parrott

Born: 11 May 1964, Liverpool, Merseyside

Career highlights
Embassy World Champion 1991

Pontin's Junior Champion 1981
Pontin's Open Champion 1982
Junior Pot Black Champion 1982, 1983
European Open Champion 1989, 1990, 1996
Dubai Duty Free Classic Champion 1991, 1992
UK Champion 1991
International Champion 1994
Malta Grand Prix Champion 1994
Thailand Classic Champion 1995
German Masters Champion 1998
Nations Cup Team Winner 2000

LIVERPOOL has a fine tradition of providing top-class sportsmen and John Parrott, one of snooker's most instantly recognizable faces, has done much to popularize the sport both on and off the table. Brought up by his father Alan after his parents split up, he was given the chance to prove himself as a competitive player in the local Garston League. But if it hadn't been for a rainy day in Liverpool, he might never have taken up snooker in the first place. Both John and his father were good bowls players and were scheduled to play together one day during the school holidays, only for rain to curtail the match. Looking for alternative entertainment, they ventured into the Dudley Institute snooker club and John immediately took to the game.

Parrott's amateur record was to prove better than that of many peers who turned professional before him, but shrewd advisers, led by his business manager Phil Miller, encouraged him to wait before applying for professional status. John first came to national prominence in 1981, when he won the Pontin's Junior Championship and recorded the highest break (97) in the inaugural *Junior Pot Black* series, which was won by Dean Reynolds. The following year he enjoyed further success at Pontin's when he won the Open event, beating Ray Reardon in the final. As an amateur he enjoyed the luxury of a 25-point start per game and even Ray Reardon could not afford to give that away to an amateur of Parrott's stature. Also in 1982, Parrott became the first person ever to win the junior and senior Merseyside titles in the same year, incidentally becoming the youngest winner of the senior title. He also went on to win the *Junior Pot Black* title and was runner-up in the

national junior championships, adding to his two runner-up positions in the boys' championship in 1979 and 1980. Such was the interest that Parrott was attracting at this time from inside the snooker world that cue manufacturers Peradon and Fletcher arranged a contract with him to endorse their product. The contract was worth in the region of £5,000, a substantial sum for an amateur. John had hoped to leave the amateur game with the English Amateur title to his name, but, although he reached the 1983 final, he was surprisingly beaten by Chesterfield's Tony Jones. He did, however, win a second *Junior Pot Black* title before finally turning professional prior to the start of the 1983–4 season.

In his third professional tournament, the Lada Classic at the Spectrum Arena, Warrington, Parrott caused sensation after sensation. Following his elimination of Doug Mountjoy by 5–4 in the qualifying competition, he emphatically beat Alex Higgins 5–2 on his 'senior' television debut. In the next round he knocked out Tony Knowles even more decisively, 5–1. That led to a semi-final appearance against Steve Davis. In front of a large and partisan crowd – Warrington, after all, is only a stone's throw from Liverpool – Parrott won the first frame and kept edging in front by one until Davis made it 4–3. Parrott then showed great composure to come back to 4–4 only for the occasion to get the better of him as Davis ran out the 5–4 winner.

Parrott followed up a promising debut season by reaching the quarter-finals of the World Championship in 1985, but lost another great battle, 13–12, to former champion Ray Reardon. However, his first final was not far away. In 1987–8, and in the top sixteen for the first time, Parrott justified his position by reaching the final of the Mercantile Credit Classic at Blackpool. His opponent was Steve Davis, their third meeting in a ranking tournament, and, in another close affair, Davis once more emerged the winner, this time by 13 frames to 11.

In 1989 John reached the World Championship final but was well beaten by Steve Davis yet again, the score 18–3. But two years later he had his revenge over Davis in the semi-finals, and went on to his greatest achievement, capturing the Embassy World Championship. He finished the first session of the final with a massive 7–0 lead over Jimmy White and went on to win 18–11, later displaying the trophy in front of a packed Anfield, the home of Liverpool FC – an occasion that will remain long in his memory, not least since he is an avid Everton fan!

Jimmy White again fell victim to Parrott in the final of the 1991 UK Championship, going down 16–13. Parrott's victory made him one of only four players to complete the World and UK double in the same year, the others being Stephen Hendry, Steve Davis and John Higgins. Later that year, Parrott's World Championship cue was stolen from the boot of his car at

Heathrow Airport.

Ranked No. 2 in the world between 1992 and 1994, Parrott was among the world's top sixteen for fifteen seasons in a row, in eight of these being in the top four. He has won tournaments over the years in nine different countries, including majors in France, Malta, Thailand, Monaco, Belgium, Pakistan and China. He also led England to victory in the 2000 Nations Cup at the Hexagon, Reading, marshalling his troops – Ronnie O'Sullivan, Stephen Lee and Jimmy White – to a 6–4 victory over defending champions Wales. Fittingly, it was the skipper who held his nerve against opposite number Darren Morgan in the deciding frame to seal the match.

One of snooker's great ambassadors, John Parrott MBE has helped popularize the game through his role as team captain on BBC Television's *A Question of Sport* quiz show. A tireless worker for charity, the wisecracking Liverpudlian, who is also an accomplished after-dinner speaker, is fourth on snooker's all-time money list with career earnings approaching the £3 million mark.

John Pulman

Born: 12 December 1923, Teignmouth
Died: 26 December 1998

Career highlights
World Professional Champion 1957, 1964, 1965, 1966, 1968

English Amateur Champion 1946
News of the World Champion 1946, 1957
Professional Matchplay Champion 1957

ONE OF the truly great characters of the game and one of the most generous, John Pulman, or 'Pully' as he was known throughout the snooker world, was one of the sport's pioneers and was responsible with a handful of others for keeping it going during the 1950s and 1960s when it nearly folded through lack of public support.

The tall Devonian first hit the headlines in 1946 when, as a 20-year-old unknown, he beat Albert Brown 5–3 in the final of the English Amateur Championship to become the youngest ever champion. Later that year, Pulman turned professional with the backing of a Bristol businessman, Bill Lampard, at whose house he stayed and in whose billiard room he practised intensively every day. John won £400 in his first professional tournament, the *Empire News* event, and was thus entitled to compete on level terms against the 'giants' of snooker, Joe Davis, his brother Fred, and the Scottish World Champion, Walter Donaldson. Further success followed in the 1954 *News of the World* round-robin tournament, in which Pulman finished top and collected a handsome prize of £3,500, beating Joe Davis into second place from a field of nine professionals – Joe was conceding 12 points per frame to John.

Pulman's progress to World Championship glory was gradual. He gave Fred Davis a close match in the 1954 semi-final and another in the 1955 final, leading 31–29 at the start of the last day. He came to the brink of victory in the final the following year, but Davis recovered to beat him. It was not until 1957 – a year in which there were only four entries, Joe Davis not among them – that Pulman won the world title, staged in Jersey. He was unable, however, to capitalize fully on his new status as champion, for the game subsequently entered an unprecedented depression such that the championship fell dormant until it was revived on a challenge basis in 1964. That year he fought off the challenge of Rex Williams, 43–40. In accordance with the new system, Pulman had to accept a challenge from any of his professional colleagues at any time, and in March 1965 Fred Davis entered the championship stakes again. It turned out to be one of the greatest finals of all time. Played at Burroughes Hall – the best of seventy-three frames over six days – the match went the full distance.

The frame scores were level at 20–20 and 30–30, and it was a toss-up as to who would win. On the sixth and final day, Pulman won three of the first four frames in the afternoon, with Davis responding by winning three in a row to make it 33–33. When Fred took the lead at 36–35, the odds seemed heavily in his favour. One slip now and Pulman was an ex-champion. But Pulman scored an early 27, followed by a 23, and won the frame 69–40 on the pink. Thirty-six frames all and the spectators were on the edge of their seats. It was the final frame with Fred to break. Each player successfully negotiated a couple of safety shots before Fred made the first mistake, the white kissing a red near the

blue spot. John made a 32 break off four blacks. Fred then made 10 and 14 but John got back to score a splendid 33, which gave him a lead of 40 with just four colours left. There was no way Fred could pull it back; Pulman had retained his title by the narrowest of margins, 37–36.

Another championship, held in 1965, was decided on a series of matches played in South Africa, with Pulman again victorious, this time against Rex Williams, the final score being 25–22. Then, in another challenge match in South Africa, Pulman achieved his sixth successive championship win by convincingly beating the South African Freddie van Rensburg 39–12.

On his return to England in 1966, Pulman was challenged, on a best-of-seven-matches basis, again by Fred Davis at St George's Hall, Liverpool. Pulman's constant matchplay over the preceding two years gave him the edge over Fred and he won the series of five-frame matches by 5–2. The final challenge to his reign came from Eddie Charlton in the early spring of 1968. The event, as with John's first defence against Fred Davis, was once again played over the best of seventy-three frames, this time at the Co-op Hall, Bolton, and was sponsored by the tobacco firm Player's, which had done much to foster interest in snooker that season. Pulman went on to win 39–24.

The World Championship was restored to a knockout basis in 1968–9, when the established players were challenged by a wave of newcomers from the amateur ranks. Pulman stood up to the test better than any of his contemporaries, reaching the world final again in 1970, only to lose 37–33 to Ray Reardon. Thereafter, his standard of play gradually declined, exacerbated by injuries sustained in a serious car crash in October 1972. John recovered, however, to show glimpses of his former quality, and in 1978 achieved his best form for some years, making it as far as the world semi-final.

Chiefly known subsequently as a television commentator, John Pulman was also unmatched as a raconteur, his sense of humour enlivening many a function. If a ball came slowly off a cushion, John would inquire 'Whatever happened to rubber?' or when one of the pockets wasn't illuminated too well by the light, he'd say to the crowds: 'Can someone strike a match as I play this shot, please . . . Jesus, did you see that ball roll off?' Playing a friendly match against his good friend Ray Reardon at the home of George Lock, an engineer, at Bourne End in Buckinghamshire, Reardon knocked in a 147. Pulman looked at Reardon and said, 'That's it then, you've just spoiled the night.' Everybody collapsed with laughter and the host said, 'Shall we play any more games?' John said: 'What else do you want to see? You can't pot any more balls than that. Get the champagne open and let's have a drink!' George ran downstairs and came back with the bubbly, after which John leant against the baulk end of the table, turned to the spectators, drank his champagne and told jokes for a full ninety minutes without stopping.

Ray Reardon

Born: 8 October 1932, Tredegar, Gwent

Career highlights
World Professional Champion 1970, 1973, 1974, 1975, 1976, 1978

Welsh Amateur Champion 1950, 1951, 1952, 1953, 1954, 1955
English Amateur Champion 1964
Pot Black Champion 1969, 1979
Pontin's Professional Champion 1974, 1975, 1976, 1978
Pontin's Open Champion 1975
Benson & Hedges Masters Champion 1976
World Cup Team Winner 1979, 1980
Welsh Professional Champion 1981, 1983
Professional Players' Tournament 1982
Yamaha International Masters Champion 1983

RAY REARDON held the sport of snooker in an iron grip throughout the 1970s. Six World Championships – four in succession – put the stamp of greatness on the laugh-a-minute Welshman, who, together with Alex Higgins and John Spencer, formed part of a colourful trio that led snooker into the television age. Yet Ray always insisted, no doubt because of his experiences as a young man working down the mines, that 'Snooker's just a game. It isn't a matter of life or death.'

At the age of 14, Ray followed in his father's footsteps by becoming a coalminer. Already interested in snooker, he used to protect his hands while down the mine by wearing white gloves. The caution paid off – in 1949 he won the *News of the World* amateur title at the age of 17, for which he was presented with an ash cue by Joe Davis. That cue was to be the key to his success.

During his amateur days in Tredegar, Reardon enjoyed a great rivalry with another Tredegar man, Cliff Wilson. Their meetings, in which Reardon was invariably successful, attracted large crowds and considerable betting interest. Reardon won the Welsh Amateur title six years in succession between 1950 and 1955, and it was only when the Reardon family left the area that Wilson won his first title.

Closure of the Tredegar pits during the mid-1950s had prompted the Reardon family to move to the Stoke-on-Trent area to continue life in the mines, and Reardon got a job at the Florence Colliery. In 1957, however, a mining accident led to him being buried alive for over three hours. This episode persuaded him that enough was enough and he left to join the Stoke-on-Trent constabulary. He dropped out of the amateur game for several

seasons, but returned in great style to win the 1964 English Amateur Championship from John Spencer, who was destined to become his main rival for many years to come.

Snooker was at its lowest ebb when Reardon eventually turned professional in 1967, with just a handful of professionals operating what was effectively a closed shop. There were no tournaments as we know them today and precious little prize money or exhibition work. But Ray Reardon was a fighter and when, in 1970, Pontin's offered him a summer season of exhibition matches at holiday camps, it was manna from heaven for a struggling professional. Pontin's faith in Ray was rewarded when, with renewed confidence, he won the 1970 World Championship – a prelude to the series of great battles he was to have with Alex Higgins and John Spencer throughout the 1970s, matches from which he generally emerged on top. That first World Championship victory came against John Pulman, 37–33. Ray's next title came three years later when, in one of the greatest championship recoveries ever, he fought back from 19–12 down against John Spencer to win their semi-final 23–22. In the final, he trailed Eddie Charlton 7–0 at the end of the first session, but went on to win 38–32. Just twelve months later, back in Manchester at Belle Vue, he won his third title with a comparatively easy victory over the 1974 *Pot Black* champion, Graham Miles, by 22–12. The 1975 World Championship, played in Australia, extended Reardon to the full, and this time it was no easy win for him. In the final against Eddie Charlton in Sydney, Ray won by just one frame, 31–30. In 1976, in Manchester again, he won his fifth title, beating Alex Higgins 27–16.

Thanks to the colour that Reardon, Spencer and Higgins brought to the game, the snooker revival took off in earnest. Reardon won the first edition of *Pot Black*, the one-frame weekly series. Then, in 1978, when the World Championship became an Embassy-sponsored event with a new home at Sheffield's Crucible Theatre, Reardon recaptured his glory days by winning the last of his six titles, beating Perrie Mans 25–18. Another major success that year was in the *Daily Mirror* 'Champion of Champions' Tournament at the Wembley Conference Centre, where Ray beat Alex Higgins 11–9 to win the first prize of £2,000.

By the turn of the decade, Reardon appeared to be in decline, but the game's first modern superstar was not about to go quietly. Three months of hard work in his local billiard hall paid off handsomely when, in 1982, he again reached the World Championship final, only to lose a classic encounter 18–15 to Higgins. Yet Ray still wasn't finished, later that year lifting the Professional Players' Tournament first prize and adding the Yamaha Organs International the following season, beating Jimmy White in both finals. Even then, Reardon still had a few more tricks up his sleeve.

Without doubt the greatest safety player of all time, he forced his way into the 1985 World Championship semi-finals after tying John Parrott up in knots. Three years later, after one of the most dismal periods of his glittering career, having been constantly plagued by eye trouble, he inflicted a 5–0 whitewash on world champion Steve Davis in the British Open at Derby. And in January 1989 he shocked the life out of a young Stephen Hendry in the Mercantile Credit Classic by taking him all the way in a nine-frame thriller.

In 1976 Ray Reardon was the first ever snooker player to appear on the TV show *This Is Your Life* and in 1979 he was Roy Plomley's guest on *Desert Island Discs*. He has also appeared on various chat-show programmes, including *Parkinson*, and been a panellist on *A Question of Sport*. Nicknamed 'Dracula', he was awarded the MBE in 1985. A former president of the WPBSA, he is now the Association's Chairman of Coaching and spearheads its drive to get more people interested in the sport. His philosophy is simple: 'Enjoying playing is the important thing, and you enjoy snooker more when you can play to a better standard.' Ray epitomizes the supreme professional. Few people have possessed such touch, such consistency at the highest level, and such modesty – the latter in particular having endeared him to millions the world over.

John Spencer

Born: 18 September 1935, Radcliffe, near Bury, Greater Manchester

Career highlights
World Professional Champion 1969, 1971, 1977

English Amateur Champion 1966
Pot Black Champion 1970, 1971, 1976
Norwich Union Open Champion 1973, 1974
Benson & Hedges Masters Champion 1975
Canadian Open Champion 1976
Pontin's Professional Champion 1977
Benson & Hedges Irish Masters 1978
Warners Open Champion 1978
Bombay International Champion 1979
Holsten Lager International Champion 1979
Wilson's Classic Champion 1980
Winfield Masters Champion 1980
World Cup Team Winner 1981

JOHN SPENCER learned to play snooker on a makeshift home table, consisting of a bagatelle board with twelve nails knocked into it to form pockets, and tape tied from one nail to another to form cushions. His first games on a more traditional surface were played at the Radcliffe Sunday School Institute, and it was there, at the age of 15, less than a year after his first 'proper' game, that he made a break of 115, starting with a red and a yellow and followed by 14 reds and 14 blacks.

John carried on playing until he was 18 and then retired for ten years until a friend recruited him for a local needle match. A succession of money matches, for sums between £10 and £20, followed. He won fourteen of these in succession and was persuaded to enter the English Amateur Championship, the first tournament in which he ever participated. He then proceeded to reach the final of the English Amateur Championship two years running, carrying off the title in 1966. Spencer also finished runner-up in the World Amateur Championship that year, and after another brief lay-off was accepted into the professional ranks, managing to persuade a sympathetic bank manager that he had a great chance of winning the 1969 world title at the first attempt, if only he could raise the £100 entry fee. Fortune smiled on him as he beat reigning champion John Pulman, Rex Williams and finally Gary Owen in a one-sided final to lift the £1,300 prize.

Having lost his title to Ray Reardon and then regained it in 1971, Spencer looked likely to dominate the sport, especially after winning a series

of other titles, including TV's *Pot Black* twice. But brash newcomer Alex Higgins put the brakes on Spencer's ambitions with his never-to-be-forgotten 1972 World Championship victory. It was to be Reardon who dominated the sport for the next few years, John's demise starting in the 1973 World Championship semi-final, when he let slip a 19–12 lead over Reardon and went down 23–22. As if that wasn't enough, his troubles were compounded a year later when his beloved cue was broken in four places. It had been lying beside him in the passenger seat when he was involved in a serious car crash. The cue was expertly repaired, but although Spencer won his next event it was never the same again. He subsequently hit on the idea of using a Canadian two-piece instrument, a design that was to revolutionize the manufacture of cues. The feeling in the game at the time was that nothing could beat a one-piece cue for accuracy, but Spencer was to prove the received wisdom wrong. In 1975 he became the first winner of the prestigious Benson & Hedges Masters tournament, beating Ray Reardon 9–8 in the final. A year later he won *Pot Black* for the third time. Then, in the 1977 Embassy World Championship, the first to be played at Sheffield's Crucible Theatre, he went all the way to clinch his third title, beating Cliff Thorburn in the final.

They played best-of-49 games then as opposed to today's best-of-35, and the final was spread over eight sessions. Thrilled that there was a Canadian in the final for the first time, many of his compatriots rang Thorburn to wish him well, oblivious to the time difference between the two countries. After twenty-six frames, Thorburn led 15–11 but didn't have the self-belief to pull away, and with two sessions to play, a morning and an afternoon (the timing of sessions arranged so that the climax to the event could be screened on BBC's *Grandstand*), the score stood at 18–18. Spencer won the first three frames to lead 21–18, was pulled back to 21–20, but then drew away again for a 25–21 win and a £6,000 first prize – considered a fortune at the time.

In 1979, playing Cliff Thorburn in the quarter-final of the Holsten Lager tournament at Slough, Spencer became the first player to compile a maximum 147 break in tournament play. Frustratingly for John, the break was never officially ratified because the pockets of the table did not conform to the official templates. To add to his misfortune, the cameras were not rolling at the time of his historic break because the television crew covering the event were at lunch owing to a work-to-rule. By a further irony, the tournament was one of the few competitions that did not carry a special prize for a 147 break. Imagine Spencer's chagrin when three years later, in the second round of the Lada Classic at the Oldham Civic Centre, he sat and watched opponent Steve Davis create history by making the first official competitive 147 on television. Later in 1979, Spencer, together with some of his colleagues, was invited to Bombay to compete in an international round-robin tournament sponsored by a local paint company. At the finish, John had won the first prize of £2,000, the highest break prize with a score of 108, and the Man-of-the-Series award.

During the 1984–5 season, following the shock discovery that he was suffering double vision because of an incurable eye disease, *Myasthenia gravis*, John's form deserted him and he lost his world top-sixteen ranking for the first time in a long illustrious career. He arrested his eye condition by taking steroids daily (and later participated in a parachute jump to raise money for research into the disease), but it soon became clear that he was no longer the force he had once been. With his wife Margo, John opened a luxury snooker club/restaurant called 'Spencers' in Bolton in 1985. Nowadays, he also acts as a consultant to an Internet snooker site.

A great character and a joker, John Spencer treated the game as fun. When he lost to Perrie Mans in the first round of the 1978 World Championship, the closing sequence on the BBC focused on a man fast asleep in the auditorium. The look on the face of the producer Nick Hunter when Spencer told him it was his father was one of disbelief. Commentator David Vine was in on the act, but Hunter fell for it hook, line and sinker. He kept apologizing and Spencer kept ignoring him – it was three weeks before Hunter realized it was a joke.

Kirk Stevens

Born: 17 August 1958, Toronto, Canada

Career highlights
Canadian Professional Champion 1981, 1983
World Team Cup Winner 1982

WHITE SUITS, white shoes and long hair – these were trademarks of Kirk Stevens, a player who brought an air of flamboyancy into the world of professional snooker during the 1980s.

Stevens first played snooker at the age of 10 in the Golden Cue Centre, Scarboro, Toronto, but like fellow Canadians Cliff Thorburn and Bill Werbenuik he had to move to Britain to further his career because Canadian snooker was insufficiently advanced to offer the professional player a secure livelihood. At the age of 12, Stevens is said to have challenged Cliff Thorburn, then the resident professional at a billiard hall, to a game for $2 a frame. Thorburn beat him after conceding forty points a frame, then declined Kirk's cash. But Stevens insisted, fishing out $4 from his back pocket to keep the record straight. At the age of 15 Kirk went on the road, travelling all over Canada and North America playing for money. Then, when Kirk was 18 – his parents having already split up – his mother was killed in an arson attack on her Toronto home. That experience left Stevens emotionally scarred but motivated him to succeed at something that might allow him to escape from his memories.

Kirk became a useful amateur player, in 1978 reaching the semi-finals of the World Amateur Snooker Championship held in Malta. Although he was well beaten 8–2 by Cliff Wilson, he decided to turn professional, his application being accepted in December 1978. The following year he won the Canadian Championship, beating Cliff Thorburn, the reigning champion, 7–5, and so regaining his $4 with interest! That year also saw Kirk Stevens's first entry into the World Championship, but, after beating South Africa's Roy Amdor, and then John Pulman, he was beaten 13–8 by Fred Davis. Later that year he played for the Canadian team in the State Express World Cup and reached the semi-finals of the Canadian International before losing by one frame, 9–8, to Terry Griffiths.

The inaugural Canadian Professional Championship, sponsored by Dufferin Cues, was held in 1980. Stevens reached the semi-finals only to lose 9–7 to his young contemporary Jim Wych. Later that year, he qualified for his second World Championship at Sheffield when he beat David Greaves and Mike Hallett in the qualifying rounds. The first round proper saw him beat

Graham Miles 10–3, Kirk having a break in that match of 136, tying with Steve Davis for the highest break in the championship. He had just the black ball left for a 143 and would have picked up £5,000 for setting a new championship record had he potted it, but, though he would have expected to make the shot in practice, it was a different matter in the tense atmosphere of the Crucible, and he missed the pot. He subsequently had wins over John Spencer 13–8 and Eddie Charlton 13–7, to become the youngest player ever to reach the semi-finals. There he met Alex Higgins, a player whose style was similar to his own. Although Stevens led 5–2 at the first interval, the strain of having played so many frames in just a few days finally told and Higgins drew ahead to win 16–13.

Kirk's cheerful personality had endeared him to the British snooker-loving public, and he was invited to play in the 1981 *Pot Black* competition, having helped Canada reach the final of the State Express World Cup the previous year, where they went down to Wales. His fine displays during the early 1980s – he reached the quarter-finals of the World Championships in 1982 and 1983, losing to Jimmy White and Cliff Thorburn respectively – earned him a top-ten world ranking.

Perhaps the most memorable moment of Stevens's career came in the semi-finals of the 1984 Benson & Hedges Masters at Wembley. It's not often that a player celebrates with an all-night champagne party after missing out on his first major professional final, but that's what Kirk did after his 6–4 defeat by Jimmy White. Then again, it's not every day you make a maximum break. Both players were in sparkling form, missing the occasional shot but compensating with high-speed break-making. White took a 5–3 lead but it was still anyone's match going into the ninth frame. Those who saw what followed, either live or on television, will surely never forget the way Kirk Stevens potted every ball on the table for the third ever televised maximum. His old friend and mentor Cliff Thorburn was waiting in the wings to hug him and Stevens literally danced around the arena sharing his good fortune with all and sundry.

Despite the money he earned from the game in the early 1980s, Stevens continued to wear the same old white suit at every tournament, it not being until he signed for a London-based management group in the 1984–5 season that his wardrobe changed. The move included a contract with a leading West End tailor to promote his suits, so Stevens effectively modelled as he played! Shortly afterwards he reached his first major final, playing Silvano Francisco in the Dulux British Open – the circuit's first final without a British player – yet that match was to herald his decline. Francisco, who beat Stevens 12–9, made allegations in the tabloid press that Stevens was taking drugs, allegations that sparked a public scandal. Kirk later admitted he had a cocaine problem and, vowing to sort it out, entered a Toronto clinic for therapy and rehabilitation, but, despite a lot of sympathy, the damage had been done. Nothing, however, can take away the fact that Kirk Stevens brought a fresh approach to the game of snooker. There were many imitators but no one quite captured the imagination in the way the young Canadian did in the early 1980s.

Dennis Taylor

Born: 19 January 1949, Coalisland, Co. Tyrone, Northern Ireland

Career highlights
Embassy World Champion 1985

National Under-19 Billiards Champion 1968
National Breaks Champion 1971
Irish Professional Champion 1982, 1985
Rothman's Grand Prix Champion 1984
World Cup Team Winner 1985
Carlsberg Champion 1986
Thailand Masters Champion 1986
Winfield Masters Champion 1986
Benson & Hedges Masters Champion 1987
Carling Champion 1987

DENNIS TAYLOR was just another snooker player until 12.23 a.m. on 29 April 1985, when he became Embassy World Champion after defeating Steve Davis in one of the most dramatic matches ever played. A record 18.5 million television viewers stayed up to see Dennis, one of the most popular players on the circuit, kiss the trophy that few believed would ever be his.

Dennis started playing snooker at the age of 9 and was the local senior champion by the time he was 14. He moved to England as a 17-year-old, living with relatives in Darwen. Two years later, in 1968, he became the National Under-19 Billiards Champion, and in the 1971–2 season he gained a cap for England before turning professional in November 1972. Even in those early days as a professional he was making a name for himself as an exhibition player.

The first time the snooker public was made aware of Dennis Taylor was the 1974 Canadian Open. He reached the final after beating Alex Higgins in the semi-final but lost at the last hurdle to Cliff Thorburn. In 1975 he reached the semi-final of the World Championship, losing to Eddie Charlton, and two years later he reached the same stage again. Once more it was Thorburn who ended his chance of reaching the final. In 1979 the Irishman was in the semi-final once more, up against John Virgo, and this time he triumphed to reach the final, where he was due to meet Terry Griffiths. On paper, Dennis was clear favourite, but Griffiths, who had stunned everybody with his fine play throughout the tournament, emerged the victor, thus winning the title at his first attempt. Ranked No. 2 in the world after that event, Taylor went on to win his first Irish Professional title the following year by taking the crown from Alex Higgins. He made successful defences against Higgins and Patsy Fagan before

winning the first of the new-style knock-out championships in 1982.

Taylor caused quite a stir at the 1983 Benson & Hedges Irish Masters when he appeared wearing his new 'Joe 90' glasses, designed by former optical instrument maker Jack Karnehm. The spectacles caused Dennis to come in for some friendly banter, notably from John Spencer, but they unquestionably helped to raise his game. However, it was not until the 1985–6 season that Dennis proved himself as a winner. The death of his mother in Coalisland, Co. Tyrone, had prompted him to withdraw from the quarter-finals of the Jameson International and return to Ireland, and it was only following much persuasion by his family that he rejoined the circuit to compete in the next tournament, the Rothman's Grand Prix. Carried along on an emotional wave, he fought his way through to beat Cliff Thorburn 10–2 in the final and pocket the £45,000 first prize.

As so often happens after a first major victory, Taylor's form deteriorated for a while, but shortly before the World Championship his game improved, and he beat Alex Higgins 10–5 to regain his Irish Professional title. Sustaining the momentum, he enjoyed emphatic victories over Silvano Francisco (10–2), Eddie Charlton (13–6), Cliff Thorburn (13–5) and Tony Knowles (16–5) on his way through to the final at Sheffield's Crucible Theatre. World Champion Steve Davis was the odds-on favourite to collect yet another title, and at the start of the match there seemed little but humiliation in store for the Irishman as he went 8–0 behind. But he won seven of the next eight frames to finish 9–7 down at the end of the first day's play. The next day saw Davis forging ahead, only for Taylor to draw back to 11–11. Davis then won the next two frames on the black, taking the score to 13–11 by the end of the afternoon and edging ever nearer to his second world title. The next session saw Davis move into a three-frame lead before excellent break-building produced scores of 61, 70, 57 and 79 to gave Taylor four frames out of the next five and level the match at 15–15. Davis responded by taking two more frames in succession to make it 17–15, only for Taylor to win the next two frames, tying the score at 17–17 and setting up a last-frame decider.

The final frame lasted sixty-eight minutes and was the longest of the entire championship. Taylor forged ahead by 29–19 but then went in off a red, and Davis, despite missing a blue, came back to squeeze in front at 59–44. With just the colours to go, Davis took the green but then presented Dennis with the chance he needed on the brown. It wasn't an easy shot but it went in, and blue and pink followed to leave Taylor just three points behind at 62–59. It was now all on the black – and the black was safe. Taylor attempted a double and missed, Davis missed and then Taylor went for a long attempt that also failed. With a great chance to win the match, Davis missed again. Taylor powered the black into the pocket, raised his cue two-handed above his head, and celebrated the most memorable triumph in snooker history.

As World Champion, Taylor was financially secure for life, signing a five-year contract with Matchroom supremo Barry Hearn to look after his business interests. Though he later slipped down the world-rankings list, he enjoyed considerable success in non-ranking tournaments, winning the Benson & Hedges Masters in 1987 and, at the start of the 1987–8 season, tournaments in Japan, Canada, Ireland and England. He was also a member of the Irish team that completed a hat-trick of wins in snooker's World Cup Team during the same year.

It is easy to see why the jovial Irishman, who retired from professional snooker in 1999, is so popular. He has entertained snooker fans throughout the country with his Embassy Snooker Roadshow 'An Evening with Dennis Taylor', while his quick wit and impish sense of humour have made him an ideal man for exhibitions. Like many of his fellow professionals, he has also devoted many spare hours to raising money for charity. A great character, he will forever be remembered not only for his World Championship triumph but also as the man who put a smile on the face of the game.

Cliff Thorburn

Born: 16 January 1948, Victoria, British Columbia, Canada

Career highlights
Embassy World Champion 1980

North American Champion 1971, 1972
Canadian Open Champion 1974, 1978, 1979, 1980
Pot Black Champion 1981
World Cup Team Winner 1982
Benson & Hedges Masters Champion 1983, 1985, 1986
Winfield Masters Champion 1983
Goya Matchroom Champion 1985
Scottish Masters Champion 1985, 1986

ABANDONED as a baby by his mother and brought up by his father and grandmother in Victoria, British Columbia, Cliff Thorburn learned life the hard way – both on and off the table. He developed his talent for snooker in the late 1960s and early 1970s, playing in the pool halls of Canada and the United States, and subsequently went on the road, living the life made familiar by films like *The Hustler* and *The Colour of Money*, where you either won or didn't eat. It was a tough life but one that saw him go on to win the World Championship and to become the most successful non-British player in snooker history.

In 1970, on the death of George Chenier, Thorburn took over the crown as Canada's leading snooker player, even though he had only been playing for just over a year. At that time he had never tested his skills against the best players in the world, but the following year John Spencer visited Canada and played Thorburn in three exhibition matches. Spencer, one of the world's leading players at that time, won all three matches, but Thorburn proved a worthy opponent.

Turning professional after having won the Canadian and North American titles, Thorburn made his way to England for the 1973 World Championship, beat Dennis Taylor in the first round, but lost 16–15 to Rex Williams in the next. In the years that followed, commuting regularly across the Atlantic, Thorburn earned a reputation as one of the toughest competitors in the game. Nicknamed the 'Grinder' for his uncompromising style of play, he reached the first of his three World Championship finals in 1977, where his opponent was John Spencer. At one point, the scores were level at 18–18, but then Spencer drew ahead to take the match 23–21. The following year Thorburn won the $6,000 first prize in the Canadian Open at the Canadian National Exhibition Centre in Toronto by beating the young Londoner Tony Meo 17–15. An audience of around 1,500 watched the exciting final in the

packed match hall. Cliff not only won the title but also became the first Canadian to have his name inscribed on the trophy.

The highlight of Cliff's career came in 1980 when he played and beat Alex Higgins in the World Championship final at the Crucible. Suffering from the after-effects of a heavy cold, he went into the match very much the underdog against Higgins, who had beaten Cliff's fellow-countryman Kirk Stevens in the semi-final. When Alex opened up a 9–5 lead on the first day, the writing seemed on the wall, but Higgins, who had played controlled snooker up to that point, couldn't help but play to the gallery and Cliff punished him by winning four frames in a row to draw level. Television coverage was interrupted the following day as the BBC broadcast live pictures of the SAS storming the Iranian Embassy to bring days of siege to an end. The action on the green baize was almost as explosive and if snooker fans had not been aware of Thorburn before then, they certainly were afterwards as he carved out an 18–16 victory.

Cliff subsequently decided to make Britain his permanent base, but the move backfired and after two disappointing seasons he decided to return to Toronto. His game immediately began to improve and he won the Benson & Hedges Masters at Wembley in 1983, the first of three Masters titles. When he next returned to Britain, his determination, concentration and ability to perform under pressure took him to a series of memorable victories in the 1983 World Championship. In the second round he was up against Terry Griffiths, and, with both players acknowledged as two of the slowest on the circuit, a lengthy match was always in prospect. What they supplied, however, was the longest game in snooker history, Thorburn's 13–12 victory taking an amazing 13 hours 15 minutes. The final session of 6 hours 25 minutes was similarly the longest on record, and by the time Cliff had struck the winning ball the clock registered a mind-blowing 3.51 a.m., the latest finish ever to a professional tournament. That epic match played a significant role in the outcome of the championship, for two further gruelling encounters with Kirk Stevens (13–12) and Tony Knowles (16–15) left Cliff physically and mentally exhausted, and he went down 18–6 to Steve Davis in the final. The Griffiths match, however, was notable for more than simply its length. Attempting to pot an opening red in frame four of the match, Cliff saw the ball cannon into another red and send it across the table and into the opposite pocket, a fluke shot that was to set him on his way to a £10,000 jackpot as the first man ever to compile a World Championship maximum.

During the 1984–5 season, Thorburn became the most consistent player on the circuit. Runner-up in the Rothman's Grand Prix to his great friend Dennis Taylor, he was also beaten finalist (with Willie Thorne) in the Hofmeister World Doubles Championship, losing to Jimmy White and Alex Higgins. A third runner-up position followed when he lost to another great friend, his doubles partner Willie Thorne, in the final of the Mercantile Credit Classic. That season also brought about personal tragedy when his manager, Darryl McKerrow, was killed in an accident while on a hunting expedition in Manitoba. The loss affected Thorburn more than it might have seemed, and his Benson & Hedges victory was dedicated to his ex-manager and former friend.

Thorburn's sportsmanship, service to snooker and unofficial ambassadorship for Canada resulted in his being presented with the Order of Canada in 1984. This high point, however, was to be followed by a low when, during the MIM Britannia British Open in 1988, Thorburn failed a random drugs test. For this he was fined £10,000, banned from two world-ranking tournaments and stripped of two points from his total in the ranking list. It was a testing time for Thorburn and his family, but, typically, he gritted his teeth and took the flak to reach the semi-finals of the 1988 World Championship. He continued to play on the professional circuit until 1997, and his style of play was invariably methodical, calculated and cool.

Willie Thorne

Born: 4 March 1954, Leicester, East Midlands

Career highlights
National Under-16 Billiards Champion 1970
National Under-16 Snooker Champion 1970
National Under-19 Billiards Champion 1971, 1972, 1973
National Under-19 Snooker Champion 1973
Pontin's Open Champion 1980
Pontin's Professional Champion 1984
Mercantile Credit Classic Champion 1985

WILLIE THORNE was acknowledged by his fellow professionals and the public alike as one of the most fluent break-builders in the game. Nicknamed 'Mr Maximum', he knocked in 147 breaks on the practice table with almost nonchalant ease, achieving well over 100 of them, but unfortunately, the man with the most famous 'crown' in snooker had difficulty reproducing practice form on the match table, his record in consequence hardly reflecting his undoubted ability.

Thorne started playing snooker at the Anstey Conservative Club near Leicester when he was 13 years old, making his international debut just four years later. He won the National Under-16 Billiards Championship in 1970 and the following year went on to win the first of three successive under-19 titles. Runner-up in the under-16 snooker final in 1969, he won it the following year and in 1973 added the under-19 title to his already impressive list of junior honours. He nearly won the senior amateur championship in 1975 but lost to Sid Hood in the final. Later that year he took part in the Canadian Open, where he lost in the semi-finals to John Pulman, but he left his mark on the event, beating John Spencer 9–7 in the quarter-final.

Thorne turned professional in 1976, and when he was invited to compete in that year's *Pot Black* competition, he was, at 21, the youngest ever competitor in the event. His first win as a professional came in the 1980 Pontin's Open, when he beat fellow professional Cliff Wilson in the final after conquering Steve Davis on the way there. The following year he reached the Pontin's Professional final and led Terry Griffiths 5–1 before going down 9–8. His best ever World Championship was 1982, when he reached the quarter-final. Although he lost there to Alex Higgins, he managed to make a break of 143 in doing so – his highest in tournament play and the second-highest ever in the World Championships. The remainder of 1982 was not the best of times for the former tic-tac man, bookie's runner and photographic model: he broke both legs below the knee in a go-karting accident during the summer

and was thus forced to withdraw from the Jameson International. He continued to play snooker, however, despite his injuries and in a practice match registered a maximum 147 break – the only man to have done so with both legs in plaster!

With his friend Cliff Thorburn, Thorne came back to reach the 1984 World Doubles Final only to lose to Alex Higgins and Jimmy White. In the same year he won the Pontin's Professional title – the title that had eluded him three years earlier – beating John Spencer in the final.

When Willie reached his first major individual final in 1985, the list of spectators in the large crowd read like a *Who's Who of Sport*. In the audience for his confrontation with Cliff Thorburn in the final of the Mercantile Credit Classic at the Spectrum Arena, Warrington, were Gary Lineker, Phil Neal, Tessa Sanderson and Tony Sibson, each a personal friend of Willie as well as a fan of the sport. Lineker, one of Thorne's closest friends, was a regular practice partner at the time at Thorne's Snooker Centre in Charles Street, Leicester. Also present at the match were members of Willie's beloved Leicester Crazy

Gang – a collection of characters from his native town who rejoiced in names such as Racing Raymond, Relentless Reg, Bill the Dip and Creamcake!

Having previously edged out Steve Davis 9–8 in the semi-final, Thorne set the ball rolling with a break of 72, only for Thorburn to bounce straight back with a 77. Thorburn also took the next game despite Willie making a 52 break, and then, early skirmishes out of the way, both players proceeded to blitz the balls. Thorne started it with an 88, added a 105, then followed with a 118 clearance after initially fluking a red. The Canadian rattled home a 40, then a 75 and a 48 in one frame, and then a 72 and a 66, before ending a magnificent day's play with a 100 clearance to be just one frame behind at 8–7. TV commentator John Pulman was heard to say, 'That was the highest-quality snooker I've ever seen in a final!' The following day, Cliff and Willie shared the opening two frames, but, as the tension mounted, Thorne imposed his will on the match with the finest display of his career, forcing Thorburn into cat-and-mouse safety exchanges and actually grinding down the Grinder. Errors crept into the Canadian's play and Thorne crept towards the winning post, taking frame after frame with a clever mixture of attack and defence to win 13–8.

That long-awaited victory should have been the launch pad for bigger and better things, but the year was to end in heartbreak. Willie finished runner-up to Thorburn in the Langs Scottish Masters, then reached the final of the Coral UK Open at Preston's Guild Hall, beating Paddy Browne, John Virgo, Cliff Thorburn, Terry Griffiths and Dennis Taylor along the way. In the final he produced a brilliant exhibition of potting as he built a handsome lead against Steve Davis, and it seemed that at long last he was going to turn his talent into trophies. However, a careless miscue on the blue cost him a 14–8 lead and shattered his brittle confidence. Davis went on to win eight of the last nine frames to pull off an unlikely 16–14 victory.

Thorne reached two more ranking finals in 1986–7 but lost them both, Davis beating him again in the Dulux British Open, this time by a 12–7 margin, and Jimmy White triumphing 9–5 in the Benson & Hedges Irish Masters. Willie did, however, manage to win the Camus Hong Kong Masters and the Matchroom Trophy, the latter after joining Barry Hearn's Matchroom organization.

It was at Preston in 1987 that Thorne finally made a maximum break in a major championship. It came during his fourth-round match against Tommy Murphy in the pre-televised stage. It made Willie the fourth player to compile a 147 under tournament conditions, but the absence of the BBC cameras denied him a £90,000 jackpot. One of the most popular players on the circuit – elegant as he paced around the table and effortless in potting the balls – he remained an enigma throughout his career, failing to deliver the results he was so clearly capable of. He remains the most urbane commentator on the game.

John Virgo

Born: 3 April 1946, Salford, Greater Manchester

Career highlights

National Under-16 Snooker Champion 1962
National Under-19 Snooker Champion 1965
National Pairs Champion 1976
Coral UK Professional Champion 1979
Bombay International Champion 1980
Pontin's Professional Champion 1980
Professional Snooker League Champion 1984

A PLAYER of great class, John Virgo surprisingly failed to achieve regular tournament success. Lack of concentration was generally regarded as the reason, for on his day he was capable of beating any player in the world.

As an amateur, John Virgo learned his trade in the tough breeding ground of the Greater Manchester area that spawned so many fine players during the mid-1970s – Alex Higgins, Dennis Taylor, Jim Meadowcroft and David Taylor to name but some. As well as playing in several big-money matches as an amateur at Potters Club in Salford, he won the National Under-16 Snooker Championship in 1962 and the Under-19 title three years later, and played fifteen times for England. The remainder of his amateur career saw him win many north-west competitions, and in 1975 he reached the final of the Pontin's Open, but, despite receiving 25 points per frame from Ray Reardon, he lost to the latter 7–1. In 1976, the year before he turned professional, he won, with Paul Medati, the National Pairs title, beating the pairing of Billy Kelly and Dennis Hughes in the all-Manchester final. That year, John also came very close to reaching the English amateur final but lost in the northern area final to Roy Andrewartha. Two nights before his defeat by Andrewartha, he had compiled his first maximum 147 break, ironically against the same opponent.

When Virgo turned professional, the game was just starting to take off in popularity. *Pot Black* had done much to help its cause and Virgo was quick to appreciate that turning professional would ensure he was in on the 'ground floor'. However, life was certainly not easy in those early days because many other players had the same ambitions.

John made his mark on the professional game in the 1977 World Championship, the first to be held at the Crucible Theatre in Sheffield. After coming through two qualifying matches, he was pitched against fellow Lancastrian John Spencer. At the time, Spencer was one of the best players in the world, but Virgo gave him a tough match before Spencer went on to win 13–9 and eventually take the title. Virgo twice led by three frames, but

unfortunately at 8–8 he seemed to lose his confidence. However, he followed that World Championship performance by reaching the semi-final of the inaugural UK Championship at Blackpool's Tower Ballroom, losing 9–8 to the eventual winner Patsy Fagan.

Virgo was gaining a reputation for being a tough player to beat and in the 1979 World Championship he showed his best form to date. In the preliminary round he beat Maurice Parkin 9–0 and in the qualifying-round tie squeezed past Willie Thorne 9–8. In the first round, with the pace getting hotter, he beat Cliff Thorburn 13–10 and another Canadian, Bill Werbenuik, 13–9 in the quarter-finals. In the semi-finals of the World Championship for the first time in his career, he finally went down 19–12 to Dennis Taylor, the latter having led at the end of each of the five sessions. In the twenty-eighth frame, John came close to the first 147 in the championship, after potting twelve reds and eleven blacks, but he failed on the twelfth black. 'If I'd got that he could have had the Championship,' Virgo commented afterwards. In the play-off for third place between the two losing semi-finalists, Eddie Charlton beat Virgo 7–3. That disappointment was tempered, however, when, after a move south to join Henry West's stable, he lifted the Coral UK title at Preston's Guild Hall. After victories over Tony Meo and Steve Davis, followed by an avenging win over Dennis Taylor in the semi-finals, he beat the then world champion, Terry Griffiths, in the final but not before giving his supporters – and himself – a few heart-stopping moments. Leading 11–7 at the start of the final session and only needing three frames for victory, he was twenty minutes late. Under the rules, he was penalized two frames which made the score 11–9. Griffiths then won the first two frames of the session to level the scores at 11 all, but Virgo managed to come back eventually to win 14–13 and thus take his first major professional title.

Virgo maintained his new-found form into the following year, winning the 1980 Bombay International Tournament against Cliff Thorburn shortly afterwards by 13–7 in a two-day final. He then won the £2,000 first prize at the 1980 Pontin's Professional Tournament at Prestatyn, beating Fred and Steve Davis and then Ray Reardon in the final 9–6, which included a 96 clearance in the Virgo winning frame. In October of that year, at the New London Theatre, he beat Kirk Stevens, Dennis Taylor, Steve Davis and Ray Reardon in Group 'A' of the 'Champion of Champions' tournament. In the final, both he and Doug Mountjoy missed several frame-winning chances before Mountjoy eventually secured victory 10–8. A spell in the wilderness followed and it was not until the 1982 Jameson International that Virgo reached a major semi-final again, but this time his efforts were thwarted by David Taylor, who beat him 9–5.

Virgo was regularly in the top sixteen for most of his career, but poor results saw him drop out of that elite club in 1984. He was still playing well,

ut when it came to the ranking tournaments he wasn't picking up the
oints. He did reach the final of the Australian *Winfield Masters* in 1984 and
hen won the inaugural Professional Snooker League, but, as well as
arrying no ranking points, the latter also carried no prize money.
levertheless, it was a creditable win, achieved against other top-ranked
layers. Throughout the tournament he lost just one match – to Eddie
harlton – and he was the last man to lose his 100 per cent record. Going
ato the final match against Tony Knowles at Kelham Hall, Newick, Virgo
vas lying third but knew a win would make him champion, and in a
ervous encounter he beat Knowles 6–4 to clinch the title by a point from
ddie Charlton and Dennis Taylor.

Virgo arrested his slide down the rankings list when, in 1986, at the Dulux
ritish Open, he reached his first ranking semi-final since 1982, finally losing
–4 to Willie Thorne. A year later, in the same event, he beat Steve Davis
–4 – the first time Davis had failed to reach the televised stage of a
rofessional tournament.

Appointed Chairman of the WPBSA, Virgo has since devoted much of his
ime to the commercial sponsorship negotiations and administrative problems
f the ever-expanding professional tour, as well as providing expert
ommentary for television. Towards the end of his career, he also regularly
o-hosted the BBC series *Big Break* with Jim Davison, where his hilarious
abaret impressions of his fellow professionals earned him as much if not
nore recognition than his achievements on the table did.

Bill Werbenuik

Born: 14 January 1947, Winnipeg, Canada
Died: 22 February 2003

Career highlights
Canadian Professional Champion 1973
North American Champion 1973, 1974, 1975, 1976
World Cup Team Winner 1982

WHO WAS the first man to split his trousers during a live television broadcast? Which snooker player was allowed to set £2,000 worth of lager against his income as a tax-deductible item? Which snooker player lived in a mobile home? And who was the heaviest professional snooker player? The answer, of course, is Canadian Bill Werbenuik.

'Big Bill' was born in Winnipeg, later moving to Vancouver, where he started playing snooker at the age of 9. He won the Canadian Amateur title in 1973, and later that year turned professional. He celebrated by completing the double, consisting of the Canadian Professional Championship and the North American Championship. British audiences saw him for the first time in 1974 when he arrived for the World Professional Championship, but between then and 1978 little was seen of him on these shores. It was only after reaching the quarter-finals of the World Championship in 1978, when he lost to Ray Reardon, that Bill decided to stay in Britain and take part in other tournaments. He made his base at the North Midland Snooker Centre in Worksop, but 'lived' wherever his next tournament or exhibition took him, having luxuriously fitted out an old bus that he had purchased for £20,000. Equipped with a television, video, stereo, kitchen, shower, two bedrooms, lounge, telephone and lager on draught, he saved a fortune on hotel bills by parking this mobile home wherever he was appearing and rolling straight into bed after a night's snooker.

Bill's lager intake may have seemed excessive to some but in terms of his career it was a life-saver. He suffered from a disease known as Familiar Benign Essential Tremor, a condition that caused his right hand to shake, and the only remedy he found effective was the consumption of copious quantities of alcohol. Deeming it essential for his career, the Inland Revenue duly ruled that he could write off the £2,000 a year spent on lager against tax!

In 1979 Werbenuik reached his second World Championship quarter-final, beating the No. 4 seed John Spencer along the way. Though he lost 13–9 to John Virgo, he had the satisfaction in the eighteenth frame of equalling Rex

teve Davis looks on anxiously as Bill Werbenuik plays a shot in the Coral UK Championship of 1980.

Williams's championship-record break of 142. Had it been just one point higher, Bill would have collected a bonus cheque of £5,000. Later that year, he went on to reach his first major semi-final, losing 9–3 to Terry Griffiths in the Coral UK Championship.

In 1980, as a member of the Canadian team that played and lost to Wales in the State Express World Cup Team, Bill appeared in his first major final – but what an embarrassing tournament it was to prove for him. In an early match against England's David Taylor, his rather tight trousers split around the posterior, and what's more he wasn't wearing underpants! To cap it all the television cameras caught all the action. After an appeal was made for a needle and thread, Bill had to leave the arena for fifteen minutes for the necessary repairs to be made. Canadian captain Cliff Thorburn took the opportunity to crack a few jokes. 'This is a real needle match', he quipped, and 'I was hoping Bill was going to sew it up for us!'

Another quarter-final place came Werbenuik's way in the 1981 World Championship, but yet again he could not overcome that hurdle, losing 13–10 to Ray Reardon. His first major honour came in 1982 when he helped Canada beat the strong English trio of Steve Davis, Tony Knowles and Jimmy White in the final of World Cup Team competition. Werbenuik played an important role in that victory, losing only one game throughout the tournament – his very first match, against Doug Mountjoy. His 2–1 win over Davis in the final was a vital victory, the Canadians going on to win the final 4–2.

It was another two years before the popular and jocular Canadian reached his first major individual final. After beating Alex Higgins, Doug Mountjoy and Kirk Stevens in the 1983 Lada Classic, Bill, who was playing some of the most consistent snooker of his career, came up against Steve Davis in the final at Warrington's Spectrum Arena. Davis was on fire and Werbenuik did well to lose by only 9–5. In the World Professional Championship that year Bill seemed to be on course for the semi-final as he led Alex Higgins 9–7 going into the final session, only to lose 13–11. That summer then saw him reach the final of the Australian *Winfield Masters* by beating Dennis Taylor, Alex Higgins and Tony Knowles, but he was again a beaten finalist, losing to Cliff Thorburn. In that match, though, he nearly scooped the jackpot for a 147 break. Having taken fourteen reds and thirteen blacks, he missed the next black, which ironically was not all that difficult. To crown a memorable year, he was recognized as the Personality of the Year by the Snooker Writers' Association.

Having reached his highest ever ranking of eighth, Bill went into the 1984–5 season full of confidence, but it all turned sour on him. He never got beyond the second round of any tournament, and a season later he was out of the top sixteen. Apart from a losing quarter-final appearance in the 1986

Dulux British Open, the ebullient Werbenuik had little to cheer about the following season either and his slide became so great that he slipped out of the top thirty-two. By this point the tremor in his right hand had intensified, so he turned to the beta-blocker drug, Inderel, which provided some relief. After this was put on the list of drugs outlawed by the WPBSA, however, Werbenuik was fined and suspended after continuing to take it. He went home to Vancouver over Christmas 1988, commenting before flying home, 'It looks like the end of the road. There is no other drug available. I could take other medication, but I would need three times the dosage and it could possibly kill me.'

One of the game's great characters, Bill Werbenuik died in February 2003, aged 56. In his final years he had lived with his mother on disability benefits, having dismissed the modern game as 'boring'.

Jimmy White

Born: 2 May 1962, Tooting, London

Career highlights
National Under-16 Snooker Champion 1977
Pontin's Junior Champion 1978
Pontin's Amateur Open Champion 1978
English Amateur Champion 1979
Indian Amateur Champion 1980
World Amateur Champion 1980
Scottish Masters Champion 1981
Benson & Hedges Masters Champion 1984
Carlsberg Champion 1984, 1985
World Doubles Champion 1984
Benson & Hedges Irish Masters Champion 1985, 1986
Mercantile Credit Classic Champion 1986, 1991
Rothman's Grand Prix Champion 1986, 1992
British Open Champion 1987, 1992
Canadian Masters Champion 1988
European Open Champion 1992
UK Professional Champion 1992

JIMMY WHITE is without doubt one of the most talented players to have graced the game of professional snooker. His nickname 'Whirlwind' – earned for his quick-fire style of play – could hardly be more appropriate, as millions of snooker followers will readily testify.

Jimmy spent his formative years playing the snooker halls of Tooting. Formal education came a distant second best, his headmaster actually giving permission for Jimmy to take afternoons off to practise at the local billiards hall! In that uncompromising part of London no quarter was given on the table and none asked for, but there was something about the young White that set him apart. People knew even then that he was going to be a great player. He first burst on to the scene in 1979, at a snooker club in Helston, Cornwall, where he was opposed by Dave Martin in the final of the English Amateur Championship. White came through a tough match to win 13–10, becoming the youngest person ever to win the title. During the course of the match he compiled a 130 break, but unfortunately this was not ratified as a championship record because of oversized pockets. More amateur success was to follow when, aged 18, he travelled all the way to Hobart for the World Amateur Championship in 1980. White topped his group, scraped home 5–4 in the quarter-final against Steve Newbury, and beat Paul Mifsud of Malta 8–6 in the semi-final. In the final he knocked in breaks of 80 and 101 to destroy Australia's Ron Atkins 11–2. That was another landmark – he was the game's youngest ever world amateur title-

holder. He returned home via Calcutta, where he won the Indian Championship, to find that his application to turn professional had been accepted.

At 19 years 4 months, Jimmy became the youngest winner of a professional tournament when winning the 1981 Langs Scottish Masters. He followed that up a few weeks later with victory in the Northern Ireland Classic, this time beating Steve Davis in the final. He was almost immediately tipped as a certainty to beat Alex Higgins's record of 22 years 11 months as the game's youngest professional champion, but, though the world seemed his oyster, the 'youngest ever pro champ' tag was to elude him. In 1982 he was 15–14 up in his World Championship semi-final with Alex Higgins, who miraculously snatched the thirtieth frame on the black with a 69 clearance, recognized as the finest in Crucible history. Higgins added the decider and went on to beat Ray Reardon for the title. In 1984 came White's greatest chance. He had won the Benson & Hedges Masters with a 9–5 victory over Terry Griffiths and then reached the World Championship final, where he came up against Steve Davis. Handicapped by a defective tip on the first day, he roared back from a seemingly hopeless 12–4 overnight deficit, only to lose 18–16. In the same year, he teamed up with Higgins for the World Doubles Championship, the pair ending the two-year run of Davis and Meo to win the title, beating the

Runner-up Jimmy White pictured with winner Steve Davis at the 1987 Mercantile Credit Classic at Blackpool

partnership of Thorburn and Thorne in the final. It made some amends for Jimmy, who had finished as a beaten finalist with Tony Knowles in 1983.

In 1986 White won the Mercantile Credit Classic and the following year he took two ranking events – the Rothman's Grand Prix, where he beat Rex Williams 10–6, and the Dulux British Open, where he conquered Neal Foulds 13–9. After that, the titles seemed to dry up, though he burst back to form in the 1988 BCE Canadian Masters, where he beat Steve Davis 9–4.

While there have been many classic matches in Jimmy White's career, none could better his 13–12 defeat of Stephen Hendry in the second round of the 1988 World Championship. Great friends off the table, the two stars matched each other shot for shot until Jimmy finally came home 13–12. Such was the interest that traffic came to a standstill outside Sheffield's Crucible Theatre as fans left the arena after the shoot-out. Sadly for Jimmy, though he was playing some of the best snooker of his career, he went down 16–11 to Terry Griffiths in the semi-final.

It was 1990 before White battled through to the World Championship final – a feat he was to achieve for the next five years. He lost 18–12 to Hendry, who would so often be his nemesis, then in 1991 lost 18–11 to John Parrott. Whatever hurt those two defeats brought, however, was completely dwarfed by events in 1992. On the way to his third successive final, White had become the second player to compile a maximum break in the televised stages of the World Championships, his 147 coming in a first-round match against Tony Drago. He was leading Stephen Hendry 14–8, and it seemed that this was to be his year. But then the Scot reeled off ten consecutive frames to record an 18–14 victory that, as it sank in, left White stunned and disillusioned. The following year, having publicly admitted that drinking during three Crucible finals had cost him dear, Jimmy was hammered 18–5, again by Hendry, in the 1993 World Championship final. The closest he came to winning a World Championship was in 1994, when he was beaten for the third successive year by Stephen Hendry, 18–17. Everyone watching, including the holder, believed White would be champion until he failed to pot a black in the deciding frame with the victory ceremony beckoning. The following year he went out at the semi-final stage to, you've guessed it, Stephen Hendry.

Given so many heartbreaking defeats, and over a decade without a major title – in 2001 he failed to qualify for the Crucible, losing to Irishman Michael Judge in a qualifying round – Jimmy White could be forgiven for agreeing with those who claim he is destined never to become World Champion. Despite so many setbacks, however, the father of five and 'People's Champion' is still one of snooker's biggest crowd-pullers, and he remains convinced that the elusive championship is still within his reach.

Mark Williams

Born: 21 March 1975, Cwm, Gwent

Career highlights
Embassy World Champion 2000, 2003

Regal Welsh Champion 1996, 1999, 2002
Rothman's Grand Prix Champion 1996, 2000
British Open Champion 1997
Benson & Hedges Masters Champion 1998, 2003
Irish Open Champion 1998
Liverpool Victoria UK Champion 1999
Thailand Masters Champion 1999, 2000, 2002
China Open Champion 2002
UK Challenge Champion 2003

ONLY THE THIRD player to win the UK Championship, the Masters and the World Championship titles in the same season, Mark Williams not only triumphed in the 2003 World Championship but, at the time of writing, is back on top of the world rankings, Ronnie O'Sullivan's first-round exit and Williams's quarter-final win over Stephen Hendry having ensured that the Welshman would return to the No. 1 spot. He is only the second player to regain pole position in the rankings, emulating Ray Reardon's 1982 feat.

Williams, from the former mining village of Cwm not far from Ebbw Vale in the now-redundant coalfields of South Wales, is immensely proud of his family roots. As a youngster he took up boxing, but snooker soon put paid to a career in the ring and in 1992, at the age of 17, he turned professional. The Welshman, who still practises at the Emporium, the Bargoed club where he learned his trade, failed to get past the qualifying-round stage in his first four World Championships, but his career as a whole was anything but slow-starting.

Fittingly, it was the Regal Welsh Open in 1996 that provided Williams with his first ranking title when he beat John Parrott 9–3 to become the first Welshman to capture the crown. Shortly afterwards he collected his second 'major' when he won the Rothman's Grand Prix in Bournemouth, defeating Euan Henderson 9–5 in the final. During the course of that tournament, the lightning-fast potter recorded a break of 138 – the highest of the televised stages – though his highest at that time was still a break of 142 made in 1994 in the Strachan Challenge. In April 1997 Williams became the British Open Champion, beating Stephen Hendry in the final, the 9–2 margin being Hendry's heaviest defeat in a final. The 1997 World Championship saw a

brief interruption in his run of success, when Williams, having sent Terry Griffiths into retirement with a 10–9 first-round defeat, lost to Hendry 13–8 in round two. The following year, however, trailing Hendry 9–6 in the final of the 1998 Masters, he thrilled a full house at Wembley – and 8.5 million viewers on BBC2 – by pulling back to 9–9 and then clinching a remarkable 10–9 victory on a re-spotted black – conclusive proof of his ability to cope with the intense pressure associated with top-class snooker.

During the 1998–9 season, Williams demonstrated what a formidable player he is by winning three world-ranking events in a single season. Having lost 6–4 in December 1998 to John Parrott in the German Masters, he flew from Frankfurt to Dublin and promptly won the Irish Open, making a century break in each of his five matches. Then, in January 1999, he joined Darren Morgan, Dominic Dale and Matthew Stevens in winning the inaugural Nations Cup for Wales, before heading to his native country for the Regal Welsh. Playing some memorable snooker during that event, he ended it by defeating Stephen Hendry 9–8 in a thrilling final to complete the Irish/Welsh back-to-back feat. His third ranking win of the season came in Bangkok, where he beat Alan McManus 9–7 to clinch the Thailand Masters title.

Williams was to end the following season as the world No. 1, and there could be no doubt he had earned it. As well as winning the Liverpool Victoria UK Championship and Thailand Masters, he also finished runner-up in the Champions Cup, Grand Prix, Malta Grand Prix and Regal Scottish, and so, when he arrived at the Crucible for the 2000 World Championship, he was already assured of top spot in the rankings. He went on in that tournament to beat John Read (10–4), Drew Henry (13–9), Fergal O'Brien (13–5) and then John Higgins (17–15), which took him through to the first ever all-Welsh final, in which he defeated Matthew Stevens 18–16 after trailing 13–7 at one stage. It was the closest Crucible final since Stephen Hendry had defeated Jimmy White 18–17 in 1994, Williams showing nerves of steel to become the first left-hander to lift the trophy in the then 73-year history of the competition. In so doing, he joined an exclusive club, only four other players – Ray Reardon, Steve Davis, Stephen Hendry and John Higgins – having previously achieved the perfect double of being World Champion and World No. 1 at the same time.

Williams started the 2000–1 season almost 10,000 points ahead of his nearest rival after becoming only the third player to win the UK and world titles in the same season. His victim in the 1999 UK final at Bournemouth had once again been Matthew Stevens, the score 10–8, and after also winning the 2000 Rothman's Grand Prix at Telford, where he beat Ronnie O'Sullivan 9–5 in the final, Williams unsurprisingly arrived at the Crucible for the 2001 World Championship as No. 1 seed as well as first in the world rankings. He was to succumb, however, to the Crucible curse that seems to affect all first-time winners of the trophy, losing an epic second-round match against Northern Ireland's Joe Swail, 13–12.

After going seventeen months without a ranking tournament title – a barren spell that included a 10–9 defeat by Paul Hunter in the Masters Final at Wembley – Williams ended the drought with back-to-back victories in the China Open and Thailand Masters. At Shanghai he beat surprise finalist Anthony Hamilton 9–8, coming from 8–5 behind to take the last four frames. He then completed the unique Asian double by beating Stephen Lee 9–4 in Bangkok. Sadly, though, his campaign ended in disappointment when he lost in the second round of the 2002 World Championship at the Crucible to Anthony Hamilton. The Welshman decided to follow the lead of Stephen Hendry and work with Terry Griffiths on turning his game around. This proved a resounding success, as Williams reproduced his best form in 2002–3, beating Ken Doherty 10–9 in a gripping conclusion to the Powerhouse UK Championship in York and then securing an emphatic 10–4 victory over Stephen Hendry in the final of the Masters at Wembley. Then in the 2003 World Championship Final, he survived an amazing Ken Doherty fightback to win 18–16 and take his second world title in one of the tournament's best ever finals. Ken Doherty produced a spellbinding session on the Monday afternoon, recovering from an 11–5 deficit to level at 12–12. Williams looked bewildered but, despite the tension, recovered his poise as the pair swapped frames to move to 14–14. The Welshman moved 16–14 ahead but was pegged back again by Doherty, before Williams finally closed out an amazing match.

The Welsh left-hander was back as the World No. 1, and with a victory worth £270,000. Expressing his thanks to mentor Terry Griffiths for helping him to become King of the Crucible once more, Williams vowed that this time he would not let things slip as they had done after his achievement three years earlier.

Cliff Wilson

Born: 10 May 1934, Tredegar, Gwent

Career highlights
National Under-19 Snooker Champion 1952, 1953
Welsh Amateur Snooker Champion 1956, 1977, 1979
World Amateur Snooker Champion 1978
National Pairs Champion 1979

IN CLIFF WILSON, the game of snooker had one of its great characters. He was always in demand for exhibition matches, his personality and rapport with spectators making for an amusing and entertaining evening. He was also a great potter, and with the pressure of tournament play off him would regularly put together century breaks in exhibition surroundings.

Born in Tredegar, Wilson grew up alongside another genius of the snooker table, Ray Reardon. The two men used to compete in 'shoot-outs' played in front of sell-out crowds, and Cliff, one of the amateur game's leading personalities, revelled in the fierce rivalry of those contests. He emerged on the snooker circuit in 1952 at the age of 17 and twice became the British Junior (Under-19) Champion. Beating Reardon in the 1954 National Amateur Championship semi-finals, before finishing runner-up to Geoff Thompson in the final by 11 frames to 9, he soon earned the reputation of being a hard hitter of the ball with a flamboyant, exciting style; his fast, positive, accurate potting won him several amateur championships, including the Welsh Amateur Championship in 1956. When Reardon left Wales, however, moving to Stoke to pursue a career, first in the police force and then as a snooker professional, Wilson lost interest in the game. As well as having problems with his eyes, he had a wife and four young boys to support, and a secure job in a steelworks. As a result, in 1957, he gave up the game and did not pick up a cue for fifteen years! He was coaxed back into the sport by a local club team, whom he agreed to help out. The snooker bug got him once more and it was not long before he was playing to his former high standard.

In 1973 Cliff won the first of his ten international caps, following this in 1977 with his second Welsh title. Being national champion, he was eligible for the World Amateur Championship (which had not been introduced when he had last won the title). He travelled to Malta the following year for this and easily won his qualifying group, taking all eight games. In the knock-out stage of the competition he beat Paul Mifsud 5–0, Kirk Stevens 8–2 and, in the final, Bradford's Joe Johnson 11–5. He returned, therefore, to South Wales with the trophy and a bit of glory but resisted the temptation to turn professional, instead going on, in 1979, to win his third Welsh amateur title as well as the National Pairs Championship with fellow Welshman Steve Newbury. Even then he had no real thoughts of turning professional. After all, he was middle-aged, his eyesight was none too good and he had a secure job as a foreman in the steelworks. Ironically, it was an offer to compete as a 'wild card amateur' in the 1979 Benson & Hedges Masters at Wembley that probably made up Wilson's mind to leave his job and join the professional circuit. The professional association was not too happy about having an amateur in their tournament, so, after delicate negotiations, Cliff withdrew to prevent a major confrontation. A few months later, he threw in his lot as a professional and began his steady rise up the rankings, reaching sixteenth place at the end of the 1987–8 season.

Of course, one of the perks that goes with a place in the top sixteen is a spot in the Benson & Hedges Masters, so, at Wembley in January 1989, a decade after suffering the humiliation of being invited and then having to step down, Wilson took his place there by right. Cliff would unquestionably see the funny side of that. In fact, he saw humour in most situations. His booming laugh and wheezing cough (a salutary advertisement for the

sponsor's product in the Benson & Hedges Masters!) have livened up many a hospitality room and post-match press conference. Maintaining the approach of an old-style amateur, throughout his career, if things went wrong, Cliff would just laugh it off, tell a few jokes, have a couple of pints, pick up his cheque, and head off back to the Valleys.

Wilson's biggest payday came in 1984 when he reached the final of the Welsh Professional Championship for the second time in his career. Again he filled the runner-up position, but on his way to collecting the biggest cheque of his professional career – £3,200 – he beat Ray Reardon for the first time since their amateur days.

Cliff loved pleasing the crowds with outrageous attempts at long pots and doubles, much as he did in those games in Tredegar against Ray Reardon. It wasn't the end of the world to him if he lost a match he should have won. Had he been born about twenty years later, his crash-bang style of all-out attack could easily have made him one of the real superstars of the professional game. Without any trace of envy or regret, the man whose favourite pastime is deep-sea fishing, and who claims his No. 1 hobby is 'collecting betting slips', wryly observes: 'I was the Jimmy White and Alex Higgins of snooker in the 1950s. When I was a young man I was knocking in century breaks in four minutes when Jimmy White wasn't even a gleam in his father's eye.'

Although Wilson may not have enjoyed huge professional success, he brought to the game a wonderful spirit that enriched it immeasurably.

And then there's . . .

When players were chosen for inclusion in this book of snooker legends, it was inevitable that some very good candidates would have to be omitted. Deciding whom to put in and whom to leave out was difficult. The players in the following pages represent those who just failed to make the cut.

Tony Drago

Born: 22 September 1965, Valetta, Malta

Career highlights
Malta National Amateur Champion 1983

ONE OF the most exciting players in the game and undoubtedly the fastest, Tony Drago, the Maltese Tornado, lived up to his nickname when he fired his way into snooker's record books. In a match against Worksop's Danny Fowler in the third round of the Fidelity Unit Trusts International at Stoke-on-Trent at the beginning of the 1988–9 season – a match Drago won 5–2 – one of the frames lasted just three minutes, the fastest in the history of the sport. This illustrates the way Drago has always approached the game, delighting snooker audiences everywhere with the breathtaking speed of his potting.

Drago might still be playing the one-table clubs of Malta had it not been for the Essex professional Vic Harris, who was also the first to discover the exceptional talents of Steve Davis. Harris had been chosen for a London Select Team to play against Malta's finest prospects in Valetta, and it was there that he first set eyes on the Maltese prodigy. Harris played a frame against him and won easily, but he could see that Tony had been almost paralysed by nerves and so he invited him to play again the following night. With Drago still on edge, Harris decided to smash the pack up and see what the youngster could do. All of a sudden, Drago snapped into gear and started slamming balls in all over the place. Never in his life had Harris seen anyone pot balls so quickly, not even Alex Higgins or Jimmy White. It was clear to Harris that the then 16-year-old Drago needed to play in Britain to gain experience, and with the help of Maltese tour operator Carm Zerafa this was soon arranged. Drago quickly became established on the circuit, returning home to win his National Amateur Championship from the great Paul Mifsud. His long-striding action and sure-fire potting made him a huge favourite in London, where he was now based, and he made an impressive impact on the amateur scene in Britain, earning £10,000 in a little over eighteen months. There was to be disappointment though when, starting out as favourite in the 1984 World Amateur Championship, he failed to win. Ample consolation came, however, in the form of a then world-record 132 clearance in just over four minutes. With his English improving rapidly, Drago turned professional in September 1985.

Like so many of today's youngsters in the professional ranks, Tony found it difficult to adjust to the pace. Even so, he did claim the notable scalps of Eddie Charlton and Mark Wildman in his first season. That season also saw a

moment with a difference at the 1985 Embassy World Championship. Both Steve Davis and Dennis Taylor had finished their semi-final matches a full session early, leaving the organizers to fill an embarrassing gap for television. So John Virgo, whose comic impressions of fellow players had made him a great favourite, stepped into the breach, as did Ray Reardon, who donned a false grey beard. Making up the trio was the young Tony Drago, who showed no hint of nerves, despite the clowning from the two superstars, in a session of fascinating exhibition play.

In 1986 Drago came into his own with a spectacular run in the Tennents UK Championship. He tore up the form book at Preston's Guild Hall by beating Rex Williams, John Virgo and Willie Thorne to earn a quarter-final tie against Steve Davis. It should have been easy for Davis, but Drago raced into a 3–0 lead, then held on as the defending champion took control. At 8–7 down, Drago looked out of it, but he fired home a winning break to take a thrilling match to the last frame, only to miss a crucial final yellow that would almost certainly have carried him to victory. That miss haunted Malta's leading sportsman for nearly two seasons, and it wasn't until the 1988 World Championship that he burst back into the limelight, hammering former champions Alex Higgins and Dennis Taylor to reach the quarter-finals, where he again went down to Steve Davis. Another notable achievement came in 1991 when he reached the final of the Mita World Masters, eventually losing 10–6 to Jimmy White. What fans will most remember, however, is the remarkable speed of his break-building. During the 1995 UK Championship he compiled a century break in just 210 seconds. Then, a year later in the Embassy World Championship, he shared the highest televised break prize, compiling a total clearance of 144 to equal his previous highest tournament break.

In February 1997 Drago reached the final of a world-ranking tournament – the International Open at Aberdeen – for the first time. He had previously failed nine times to get beyond the quarter-final in a ranking tournament, but a victory over John Parrott changed that and he went on to beat the holder John Higgins for a place in the final, where he was well beaten 9–1 by Stephen Hendry.

Having twice held a ringside seat as James Wattana (1992 British Open) and Jimmy White (1992 Embassy World Championships) compiled 147s, the Maltese Maestro made his first maximum 147 break during the 2003 Benson & Hedges Masters. Drago, who qualified for his twelfth World Championship in 2003, is now fighting to retain his place in the game's top thirty-two.

Patsy Fagan

Born: 15 January 1952, Dublin, Eire

Career highlights
UK Professional Champion 1977
Dry Blackthorn Cup Champion 1977

PATSY FAGAN was hailed as one of the most exciting players of the mid-1970s, but his fall from glory was as dramatic as his rise to fame. One of twelve children, he was born in Dublin, but spent most of his snooker-playing days in London. Becoming the resident professional at one of the Ron Gross Snooker Centres, he first came to prominence in 1974 when he reached the final of the English Amateur Championship, losing 11–7 to Ray Edmonds. He went on to represent Ireland in the 1975–6 Home Internationals, winning two of his three matches, including one against Willie Thorne. In 1976 he was again the losing finalist in the Southern Championship but scored a record break of 115 during the competition. When he failed to reach the final of the English Amateur Championship in 1976, he decided to turn professional.

Fagan started 1977 with the first maximum of his career, achieved on his twenty-fifth birthday in January – albeit in a friendly against Dave Gilbert at the Clapton Bus Garage Social Club. He went on to defeat Jim Meadowcroft in the qualifying rounds of the 1977 World Championship before losing to Ray Reardon by 13 frames to 7 in the first round proper. The Irishman's reputation was really established later that year with victories over John Virgo and Doug Mountjoy, a fellow first-year professional, to win the title of UK Professional Champion in a contest sponsored by Super Crystalyte. A great break-builder, Fagan picked up another winner's cheque a couple of weeks later when he won the Dry Blackthorn Cup at the Wembley Conference Centre – the first snooker tournament to be played there – beating John Spencer, and then Alex Higgins in the final.

In 1978 Patsy was unsuccessful in his defence at the Guild Hall, Preston, of his UK Professional title, losing 9–7 to David Taylor in the first round. He did, however, manage to reach the quarter-finals of that year's World Championships, his progress there including a memorable first-round match with fellow Irishman Alex Higgins in which Patsy took the last frame from Higgins in a dramatic finish after each player had won twelve frames. Unfortunately for Fagan, he met veteran Fred Davis displaying his old form in the next session, and the score ended up 13–10 in Davis's favour. That was the nearest the Dubliner came to winning the world title, and indeed, apart from reaching the last eight of the 1979 UK

Championship, he never again progressed further than the quarter-finals in any tournament.

The first sign of Fagan's decline came in 1979 when he suffered a shock first-round defeat in the World Championship; his conqueror was an 'unknown' by the name of Steve Davis, who won by 9 frames to 3. He was subsequently a member of the Rest of the World team in the State Express World Challenge Cup, but neither he nor his two partners, Perrie Mans and Jimmy van Rensburg of South Africa, could make much impression on their opponents from England and Northern Ireland. He put up a better performance in the Coral UK Championship, beating Mike Hallett and Graham Miles before succumbing to Dennis Taylor in the quarter-finals. In the 1980 World Championship, it was a case of history repeating itself, as his chance of surviving the first round was destroyed once again by Steve Davis, who won 10–6. Although he again represented Ireland in the State Express World Cup, where this time he chalked up some fine individual victories, Patsy's career was on a downhill slide. To add to his problems, he suffered from a twitch, and though he stayed on the professional circuit for a good number of years, snooker spectators were never to see the popular Irishman among the winners again.

Neal Foulds

Born: 13 July 1963, Perivale, London

Career highlights
National Under-19 Snooker Champion 1982
Canadian Open Champion 1986
Scottish Masters Champion 1992

NEAL FOULDS was tipped as the man to replace Steve Davis and though he didn't reach the dizzy heights of the 'Nugget' he carried the burden well – he was modest and level-headed, and his image and attitude were both right. He started playing snooker as an 11-year-old at Greenford Conservative Club, at the time wearing glasses though he now wears contact lenses. A lot of the credit for his subsequent success belongs to father Geoff, also a professional, who sacrificed numerous personal opportunities to coach him. In 1982 Neal won the National Under-19 Championship, beating John Parrott in the final. He made his international debut later that year, and in June 1983 he was accepted as a professional by the WPBSA. By the end of his first professional season he was ranked No. 30 in the world.

That debut season started with Neal and his father making history, both reaching the first round proper of the Coral UK Championship. It was the first time a father and son had competed in the same major professional snooker tournament. The season ended with Foulds junior reaching the last sixteen of the World Championship. A first-round victory over Alex Higgins, the 1982 Champion and 1983 semi-finalist, caused quite a stir; Neal fought back twice in the later stages to earn a brilliant 10–9 victory. He impressed by showing great calm throughout the match, despite being in front of the television cameras, though this was not an entirely new experience for him, as he had appeared on *Junior Pot Black* in 1981. Sadly for Neal, he was eliminated by Doug Mountjoy in the next round, when the Welshman's safety play tied him up in knots.

Foulds capitalized on his Sheffield form in his second professional season. He started by taking the £3,750 break prize for his 140 against Bernard Bennett in the qualifying round of the Jameson International, and followed this up by appearing in the semi-final of the Rothman's Grand Prix, for which he collected a cheque for £15,000. He had enjoyed these memorable victories over Willie Thorne (5–1) and Tony Knowles (5–2) before coming up against Dennis Taylor, and although the Irishman went on to take his first major professional title, the young Foulds gained valuable experience from the match. The following season, he pushed defending champion Steve Davis all the way in their first-round match in the 1985 World Championship, missing a difficult black that would have given him a 9–8 lead with two frames to play. Then, in the third round of the 1986 English Championship, Neal met his father Geoff, the pupil beating his tutor 9–4.

Foulds won his first major title in September 1986 when, after joining Barry Hearn's Matchroom team, he beat Cliff Thorburn 12–9 in the final of the BCE Canadian Open Championship. On receiving the trophy, Foulds said: 'Everyone says to themselves "I can win a tournament" but there's a big difference between thinking it and actually doing it.' That season, he was to prove one of the most consistent players on the professional circuit. He finished runner-up to Steve Davis in the Tennents UK Open, beaten 16–7 in the final, and runner-up to Jimmy White in the Dulux British Open, losing 13–9. He was also a semi-finalist in the Rothman's Grand Prix and Embassy World Championship. But, at the Crucible, his superb season turned sour.

Neal Foulds receiving a cheque.

Foulds became embroiled in a drugs controversy after admitting he had been prescribed a type of beta-blocker by his doctor for a heart complaint. Beta-blockers had been banned by the International Olympic Committee, but Foulds was not breaking the rules of snooker as they stood at the time. Nor, as some suggested, was he seeking to gain an unfair advantage. On the contrary, he was merely protecting his health. Doctors, MPs and the Sports Council all had their say, and it was claimed that players who took beta-blockers were cheating. Neal was a shy retiring person, and not surprisingly the injustice of the situation and the adverse publicity that followed it had a lasting and detrimental effect on him.

Despite reaching the final of both the English Championship and the Benson & Hedges Irish Masters, earning £135,560 prize money in so doing, Foulds failed to live up to expectations in the 1987–8 season, his enjoyment of snooker having been tarnished by the drugs controversy. He went on to explain: 'I never dreamt I could play the level of snooker I did two seasons ago. Now I have come to terms with the fact that I may not be able to play so consistently well again in the future. But hopefully, after the bad times I have had, I will emerge as a better player and a better person for it.'

Foulds has remained on the professional circuit now for over twenty years and only dropped out of the top thirty-two some five years ago. Nicknamed 'Buzby' for the amount of time he spends on the phone, he practises at the Ealing Snooker Centre in West London. Away from the table, his favourite hobby is greyhound racing, and he spends many an evening watching his dogs run at Wembley Stadium. Sadly, his ambitions of winning the Snooker World Championship and the Greyhound Derby seem to have passed him by.

Silvino Francisco

Born: 3 May 1946, Cape Town, South Africa

Career highlights
South African Amateur Champion 1968, 1969, 1974, 1977
Dulux British Open Champion 1985

DESPITE two impressive qualifying round wins of 9–0 and 9–1 over Chris Ross and Paddy Morgan respectively, Silvino Francisco was 250–1 to win the 1982 World Championship. Those were fair odds, of course, bearing in mind that he was little known at the time outside South Africa, but victories in the competition proper over Dennis Taylor and Dean Reynolds sent those odds tumbling as he prepared to meet Ray Reardon in the quarter-final. The 'fairy story' ended there, however, as Reardon put Francisco out of the competition.

Silvino started playing snooker when he was 9 years old. His father, a Portuguese fisherman, had moved to South Africa and bought a restaurant there, on the premises of which there happened to be a couple of snooker tables. Silvino and his older brother Mannie spent innumerable hours on these, practising and perfecting their game. Both Mannie and Silvino became leading amateurs at billiards and snooker, Mannie reaching the final of the 1971 World Amateur Billiards Championship and the final of the World Amateur Snooker Championship the following year, finishing runner-up on each occasion. Silvino never managed to scale such heights in the amateur game: his best World Amateur Championship result came in Johannesburg in 1976 when, after beating Mannie 5–1, he went on to reach the semi-finals before losing to the eventual winner, Doug Mountjoy, 8–2. However, Silvino had ambitions of turning professional, and this he did in 1978 shortly after winning his fourth South African Amateur title.

After a few years, he decided to quit his part-time job with an oil company and move to Britain in order to play snooker full-time. He did that midway through the 1982–3 season, and after his tremendous performance in reaching the quarter-finals of his first World Championship he got a job the following summer working the Pontin's circuit, which enabled him to play snooker and get paid for it – the stuff of dreams for the South African.

Based in the Chesterfield area of Derbyshire, Francisco started to make significant inroads into the professional game. He reached the semi-final of the Jameson International in 1984, where he lost to Bolton's Tony Knowles,

and later that season he made it to his first ranking final when wins over
Jimmy White, Tony Meo and Alex Higgins pitched him in the Dulux British
Open final against Kirk Stevens. That was the first ranking final not to
contain a British competitor and also the first final in which the prize for
first place reached the £50,000 mark. Kirk Stevens, by virtue of his semi-
final win over Steve Davis, was favourite to take the title, but Francisco
knocked in breaks in excess of 40 in each of the first five frames to take a
5–0 lead. The South African also had a 41 break in frame six, but Stevens's
60 was enough to get him on the scoreboard. He won the next as well to
trail 5–2 at the end of the first session. The opening frame of the evening
session lasted over an hour, Francisco finally winning it after a fluked pink.
Neither player was playing to his full capacity, and the highlight of the
evening session came in the final frame when Stevens compiled a break of
108, but Francisco still led 9–5 at the end of the first day. The Canadian
took the opening three frames of the second day to pull within one frame of

Francisco, but then luck stepped in, a couple of flukes helping the South African to take an 11–8 lead, needing just one more frame for victory. Two frames later, Silvino was the inaugural British Open Champion. The win earned him £50,000, a perfect wedding present for the South African and his bride of less than two months. Sadly, however, the final left a sour taste in the mouths of both players, and generated considerable adverse publicity for the game itself. Francisco accused Stevens in the tabloid press of having played the final while under the influence of an illegal stimulant. He was fined a record £6,000 by the WPBSA for making such a claim, and had two ranking points deducted, although when Kirk later admitted his addiction to cocaine the fine was reduced.

Silvino proved strong enough to cope with the enormous media attention subsequently thrust upon him. A large part of his Dulux winnings was spent on building an extension to the Francisco home, needed to house Silvino's personal snooker table. He spent countless hours practising, developing a part of his game that he felt was weak – his safety play. Gradually, he became an extremely tough competitor and very difficult to beat. The British Open win elevated him for the first time into the top sixteen in the world and his consistency kept him there for a good number of years afterwards. He continued playing on the circuit until 1998. Unfortunately the Kirk Stevens affair affected his game for a while afterwards, but eventually he began to produce the performances expected of him. Away from snooker, Silvino enjoys scuba diving and fishing.

Paul Hunter

Born: 14 October 1978, Leeds, West Yorkshire

Career highlights
Regal Welsh Champion 1998, 2002
Benson & Hedges Masters Champion 2001, 2002
British Open Champion 2003

PAUL HUNTER became one of the youngest ever winners of a world-ranking tournament when he captured the Regal Welsh title at the expense of John Higgins in 1998. Coming from 3–0 down in his opening match against Paul Wykes to win 5–3, he then proceeded to beat top-sixteen ranked players Steve Davis, Nigel Bond, Alan McManus and Peter Ebdon before defeating Higgins in the final. Hunter had first shot to prominence two years earlier in the same competition when, aged 17, he reached the semi-finals. Also in 1996, he had lost 9–5 to Stephen Hendry in the quarter-finals of the UK Championships after leading 5–3. When asked whether he thought Hunter had a promising career ahead of him, the Scot replied: 'He's got the game and he's got the bottle.'

After his success in the Regal Welsh, the snooker world lay at the feet of the 19-year-old Yorkshireman, but he failed for some time to follow up that memorable night in Newport, allowing himself to be distracted by the sort of off-the-table pleasures enjoyed by most teenagers. It wasn't until 1999 that he reached the televised stage of the Embassy World Championship, a 10–5 win over Euan Henderson in the final qualifying round setting up a first-round meeting with Stephen Hendry. He pushed the Scot all the way, leading 7–6 and 8–7 before losing the last three frames. His reward was a rise of twelve places in the world rankings but he failed to build on that during the 1999–2000 season.

The following year brought better things. Beaten 9–2 by Ken Doherty in the 2001 final of the Regal Welsh, he went on to capture the Masters title at Wembley plus a winner's cheque for £175,000. A semi-final victory there over seven-times Embassy World Champion and six-times Masters Champion Stephen Hendry gave Hunter the belief that he could mix it with the very best. Irishman Fergal O'Brien had made him fight all the way in the final but Hunter came back from 7–3 down to snatch the title 10–9. More than four million viewers stayed up after midnight to watch his comeback on BBC 2, the match raising his profile with both the public and the media.

In 2002, Paul won the Regal Welsh title for a second time, the Leeds youngster in the final compiling the highest break of his seven-year professional career – a total clearance of 141 in the sixth frame – to emerge a worthy 9–7 winner over Ken Doherty and finish the five-day event £90,000 richer. He subsequently became only the third player, after Cliff Thorburn and

Stephen Hendry, to retain the Masters in the 28-year history of the event with another thrilling comeback at the Wembley Conference Centre. Surpassing his performance against Fergal O'Brien the previous year, he overturned a 5–0 and 56–0 deficit against world No. 1 Mark Williams to win by the same scoreline of 10–9. That victory over Williams – his first in seven meetings – was watched by a capacity crowd of 2,516, and earned Hunter £190,000. Later that year he suffered a 10–9 first-round exit in the World Championship at the hands of Australia's Quinten Hann. In a match interrupted by a streaker wearing only a pair of socks and a mask of England football manager Sven-Goran Eriksson, Hunter, having led 5–1, was hauled back to 9–9 and then suffered a 'kick' on the white in the last frame that cost him the match.

In November 2002, Hunter won the third ranking event of his career – the British Open held at the International Centre, Telford – beating Preston's Ian McCulloch 9–4. In 2003, Hunter made a strong defence of both his Masters and Regal Welsh titles but lost in the semi-finals to Mark Williams in both competitions. Up to this point his record at the Crucible had been surprisingly poor but in 2003 he reached the World Championship semi-finals. However, despite holding a 15–9 lead over Ken Doherty and therefore being just two frames away from appearing in a World Championship final, he crashed out 17–16 as the Dubliner produced an amazing comeback. In spite of this reversal, Hunter remains upbeat and optimistic about the future: 'I really believe in myself now,' he says. 'I'm competing with the best in the world and beating them.'

The Leeds-born player recently took part in the revived series of *Superstars*, the first snooker player to do so since Tony Knowles.

Alan McManus

Born: 21 January 1971, Glasgow

Career highlights

Scottish Snooker Champion 1990
Benson & Hedges Masters Champion 1994
Dubai Duty Free Classic Champion 1994
Castrol–Honda World Cup Winner 1996
Thailand Masters Champion 1996
Coalite Nations Cup Winner 2001

TWO EMBASSY World Championship semi-final appearances during his first three seasons as a professional gave Alan McManus a spectacular start to his career. He had been voted the WPBSA Young Player of the Year for 1991, and in his first season he reached the second round of the World Championship, narrowly losing 13–12 to Terry Griffiths. His two semi-final appearances saw him lose 16–7 to Jimmy White in 1992 and 16–8 to Stephen Hendry a year later.

McManus won his first ranking title in 1994, beating Peter Ebdon 9–6 in the final of the Dubai Duty Free Classic. Another momentous occasion for him that year was his 9–0 victory over Stephen Hendry, which enabled him to win the Masters. For Hendry, who had won the Masters five times and chalked up a sequence of twenty-three successive victories in the competition, it was his first defeat at Wembley. Also in 1994 McManus took the highest break prize at the World Championship, with a total clearance of 143, one of only fifteen breaks over 140 achieved at the Crucible.

A second ranking success came for McManus when he won the Thailand Masters in 1996, again demonstrating his ability to stay cool under pressure. After successive 5–4 victories over Alain Robidoux and James Wattana, he beat Peter Ebdon 6–5 in the semi-finals and Ken Doherty 9–8 in the final. In the World Championship that year, having reached the last sixteen ever since he first played in the event in 1991, Alan beat fellow Scot John Higgins in the first round. His comments after that match typified his attitude to his profession: 'You have to knuckle down and sweat blood at this game. I used my Crucible experience to my advantage and never made things easy for him.'

After spending four successive seasons at No. 6 in the world rankings, McManus dropped four places after the 1996–7 season, his only appearance in a final being in the invitation Regal Masters at Motherwell, where he was beaten 9–6 by Peter Ebdon. It was a disappointing season, as he lost 5–2 to Ronnie O'Sullivan in the semi-finals of the Asian Classic in Bangkok and 9–1 to Stephen Hendry in the last four of the UK Championship. However, Alan was a member of the Scottish team that won the 1996 Castrol–Honda World Cup. Disappointment continued the following season when he suffered a surprise 13–10 defeat against Lee Walker in the second round of the World Championship at the Crucible, and, though he reached two finals during the course of the 1998–9 season, he lost them both, Mark Williams beating him 9–4 in the Irish Open and 9–7 in the Thailand Masters.

In January 2001 Alan rekindled his successful partnership with John Higgins and Stephen Hendry to help Scotland win the Coalite Nations Cup in Reading as they beat the Republic of Ireland 6–2 in the final. Also that season, the ardent Celtic supporter and keen cook beat his great rival Stephen Hendry 5–2 in the British Open at Plymouth to reach the semi-finals, but was then beaten 6–2 by Peter Ebdon, the eventual winner. Later that year, when he lost his first round match 10–2 to Patrick Wallace, he surrendered a proud record of having won his opening match every year since 1991 at the Crucible. It was a disastrous end to a disappointing season for the Scot, and resulted in him dropping four places down the rankings. His only semi-final appearance that year came in the British Open, although he did reach three quarter-finals.

At the start of the 2002–3 season, after beating the likes of Stephen Lee and Steve Davis, Alan reached the final of a ranking tournament for the first time in three years, going down 9–5 in the final of the LG Cup, held in Preston, to Chris Small. To date he has yet to win a ranking tournament in this country. 'It would be nice to win another ranking tournament,' he says, 'but the competition gets tougher every season. My aim now is to stay at the top of the game for as long as I can.'

Tony Meo

Born: 4 October 1959, Hampstead, London

Career highlights

Pontin's Junior Champion 1977
Warners Pro-Am Champion 1977, 1979
National Under-19 Snooker Champion 1978
Winfield Australian Masters Champion 1981, 1985
World Doubles Champion 1982, 1983, 1985, 1986
World Team Classic Winner 1983
English Professional Champion 1986, 1987
British Open Champion, 1989

BORN IN LONDON, the son of Italian parents, Tony Meo had to choose between staying in England or returning with them to their homeland. The 13-year-old decided to stay near his friends. That same year he took up snooker, after having played a number of sports but never really found one he liked. Before long, Meo's talents were spotted by Bob Davis, a Tooting taxi-driver, who took Tony and his school-mate from the Ernest Bevin Comprehensive, Jimmy White, under his wing. The pair developed fast and soon became too big for Davis to manage, so they subsequently teamed up with London's top player at that time, Patsy Fagan, under the managership of Henry West.

In 1976, aged 17, Tony Meo became the youngest person ever to compile a maximum 147, achieving this against Terry Witthread at the Pot Black Snooker Centre in Clapham. His first big win came the following year when he beat professional Doug Mountjoy 5–4 in the final of the Warners Pro-Am Tournament. That same year he beat White in the final of the Pontin's Junior competition at Prestatyn, and in 1978 he beat two-times winner of the National Under-19 Championship, Ian Williamson, to win the title. His outstanding performance of the year, however, was in Toronto, when he competed in the Canadian Open Championship and won his way through to the final against Cliff Thorburn, having defeated Alex Higgins in the semi-finals. In the final he led Thorburn 10–6 at one stage before eventually losing 17–15.

Meo turned professional in 1979, leaving the amateur ranks with a win over Jimmy White to take his second Warners Open Final. It did not take long for Tony to hit the headlines as a professional. In the 1980 Coral UK Championship – the one that gave Steve Davis his first major win – he eliminated defending champion John Virgo in the second round 9–1 only to lose to Davis in the next round.

y Meo at the table in the 1981 Coral UK Championship. He beat Alex Higgins 9–4.

In 1981 Meo came close to winning his first major competition, but he again lost to Steve Davis, this time in the inaugural English Professional Championship. In June of that year he was invited as a last-minute replacement to play in the *Winfield Masters* in Sydney – the Australian television series based on the *Pot Black* format. He returned 'delighted' after winning the event, having beaten Cliff Thorburn and John Spencer in the process. Towards the end of the year, the left-hander joined Steve Davis under Barry Hearn's management, a move that served to boost his confidence and improve his consistency. He teamed up with Steve Davis to win the inaugural World Doubles title in 1982 – Meo's first major professional win – and the pair went on to retain it the following year. That was just one of several titles in 1983, Meo beating South African Silvino Francisco to win the Pontin's Professional title at Brean Sands and proving himself an outstanding doubles player by winning the pairs title with his old school chum, Jimmy White. He then went on, with Steve Davis and Tony Knowles, to help England win the

World Team Classic, thus finishing the season as the holder of two world titles simultaneously.

One of the biggest disappointments of Meo's career came in 1984 in the final of the Lada Classic at Warrington against his stablemate Steve Davis. Trailing 7–4 at one stage, he fought back to 8–8 in their seventeen-frame match, and then, before a raucous capacity crowd at the Spectrum Arena, slowly whittled away Davis's lead in the decisive frame until, with just the colours remaining, he found himself in a winning position. But as he lined up the yellow, someone in the crowd distracted him by shouting out and he fluffed what should have been a simple shot. Davis stepped in to clear up and retain his title. Meo had another great chance to topple Davis in the Coral UK quarter-finals at Preston in December 1984. This time he led 7–4 and needed just two frames to reach his third semi-final, but Davis suddenly found his spark and reeled off five frames in a row to complete a devastating victory. In the semi-final of the 1985 English Professional Championship, Tony again led Davis, 8–7, but once more Davis proved to be his bogey-man, winning the last two frames.

Despite winning more than his fair share of trophies – he won the English Professional Championship for the first time in 1986, beating Davis in the semi-final and Neal Foulds in the final, and retained it in 1987 by beating outsider Les Dodd – one always felt that Meo should have won more. Supposed to have a brittle temperament and lack of confidence, he came out with the odd statement after defeat which he later regretted, notably his 'I'm a born loser' comment after losing to John Parrott in the 1986 World Championship. In 1989, however, Meo made his great breakthrough, just as he appeared to be on the slippery slope to oblivion. Standing a lowly thirty-first in the rankings, having slid out of the top sixteen, he burst back into the limelight during a memorable fortnight of snooker. He seemed to have hit rock-bottom just a few weeks earlier, when an administrative mix-up led to him arriving late for his match against David Roe in the European Open at Deauville, which he subsequently lost 5–1 after being penalized two games. He turned fortune on its head, however, to win the British Open Championship at Derby. After first knocking out the holder Stephen Hendry, he came back from the dead to beat Mike Hallett 9–8 in the semi-finals, and then crushed Dean Reynolds 13–6 in the final to take his first major ranking title. The £70,000 winner's cheque from the sponsors Anglian Windows was easily the biggest pay-day of Tony Meo's career, although he continued to play on the professional circuit until 1997. The money was incidental – what mattered was the recognition and respect Tony earned from everyone inside and outside the game.

Matthew Stevens

Born: 11 September 1977, Carmarthen

Career Highlights
Scottish Regal Masters 1999
Benson & Hedges Masters 2000
Travis Perkins UK Champion 2003

IT HAS taken Matthew Stevens nine years to win his first professional ranking tournament. But the new Travis Perkins UK Champion admits he might never have won one at all but for the drive and persistence of his father. Stevens dedicated the title to his father Morrell in the aftermath of a gripping 10–8 victory over Stephen Hendry at York's Barbican Centre in November 2003. And he later spoke at length about the help Stevens senior had given him during his formative years in the sport.

'If it wasn't for my dad I wouldn't be where I am today,' said the 26-year-old Carmarthen cueman. 'He took me up and down the country to tournaments and that's where I gained my experience. I started playing the game when I was about 7 and then from about 10 began to play in pro-ams. I lost most of the time, and a lot of dads might have got fed up, but he saw some potential in me and kept me going. So this win is definitely for him.'

Stevens was beaten twice in the Liverpool Victoria UK Championship Finals – in 1998 by John Higgins (10–6) and in 1999 by Mark Williams (10–8). But he then proved that he was a winner by completing a notable double. In 1999 he defeated Higgins 9–7 in the final of the Scottish Regal Masters, in doing so becoming the first winner to come through the qualifying competition. Then he struck gold in February 2000, beating Alan McManus, Jimmy White and John Parrott before overcoming Ken Doherty in the final of the Benson & Hedges Masters. Stevens, who pocketed the £165,000 first prize, staved off Doherty's comeback from 9–5 to 9–8 by compiling a break of 63 under the utmost pressure.

Also in 2000 Stevens came very close to winning the greatest prize snooker has to offer, the Embassy World Championship. Favourite to make it through to the top half of the draw after the early exits of Stephen Hendry and Ronnie O'Sullivan, he duly obliged with victories over Malta's Tony Drago (10–2), Alan McManus (13–4), Jimmy White (13–7) and Joe Swail (17–12) to take him through to the first-ever all-Welsh final with Mark Williams. Stevens looked set for victory when he led 13–7, but Williams won eleven of the next fourteen frames to emerge victorious 18–16. Stevens's consolation was a cheque for £140,000, just enough to follow Williams's lead and buy himself a Ferrari – only yellow not red!

After the final he endured a frustrating run of deciding-frame defeats, then suffered the tragic loss of his father, after which he readily admitted that 'he went off the rails'.

In the 2001 World Championships, he had impressive victories over Tony Drago (10–1) and Anthony Hamilton (13–5) before a 13–5 quarter-final victory over Stephen Hendry. However, his hopes of appearing in a second successive World Championship Final disappeared when he lost 17–15 to John Higgins in a most absorbing semi-final – the lead changing hands no fewer than eight times.

In 2002 he was once again in outstanding form in the early rounds of the World Championship, beating Mike Dunn (10–6), Jimmy White (13–3) and John Higgins (13–7) to set up a semi-final showdown against Peter Ebdon. The popular Welshman had a chance to win 17–14, but ran out of position on the last red in the thirty-first frame!

But in 2003 he finally proved he possesses a big match temperament. When he won the UK Championship, he finally lost the tag of 'best player never to win a ranking event'. His victory was another triumph for Welsh snooker after Williams's monopoly of the major prizes in the previous season. Indeed, Stevens's performance was hailed by snooker great Terry Griffiths. Griffiths has watched the new UK Champion hone his skills at the Llanelli Legend's club. 'He is a quality player and I knew his day would come. He should be in the world's top eight because he is that good.'

Rex Williams

Born: 20 July 1933, Stourbridge, West Midlands

Career highlights

National Under-16 Billiards Champion 1948, 1949
National Under-16 Snooker Champion 1948, 1949
National Under-19 Billiards Champion 1949, 1950
National Under-19 Snooker Champion 1951
English Amateur Snooker Champion 1951
World Professional Billiards Champion 1968, 1971, 1972, 1973, 1974, 1976, 1979, 1982, 1983
UK Professional Billiards Champion 1979, 1981

OUTSTANDING as a youngster, Rex Williams won seven national junior titles, including the National Under-16 Billiards and Snooker Championships of 1948, and was just 17 when he captured the English Amateur title in 1951 – the youngest winner until Jimmy White came along twenty-eight years later. From those first youthful victories right through to the present day, Rex has dedicated his life to the playing, promotion and administration of billiards and snooker.

Williams turned professional at the age of 18, unfortunately at a time when both billiards and snooker were starting their decline. Regular tournament play was limited, so he had to make his living from a few exhibition matches, supplemented by his cue-manufacturing business. Had he not turned professional there is little doubt he would have dominated the amateur scene for many years, as the latter did not decline in the same way as the professional game. However, Rex foresaw a second coming of snooker and was instrumental in reviving the defunct Professional Billiard Players' Association, which is now the World Professional Billiards and Snooker Association. He also played a big part in rekindling the World Professional Snooker Championship, which had not been played since 1952, although a World Matchplay Championship had existed until 1957.

Thus, in 1964, the World Championship was reintroduced, albeit on a challenge basis, when Fred Davis challenged John Pulman for the title. Between then and 1968 the title was contested on a challenge basis, and Williams twice challenged Pulman for the title, losing on each occasion. During his 1965 title match with Pulman, Williams created a new world championship record break of 142, which stood until 1981 when it was beaten by Doug Mountjoy's 145. He made an even better break that year, becoming only the second man after Joe Davis to register an official maximum. This came about during a match against Mannie Francisco at the Prince's Hotel, Newlands, Cape Town, on 22 November 1965.

Rex also revived the World Professional Billiards Championship in 1968, travelling to Australia to challenge the holder, Clark McConachy, who had not received a challenge since 1951. Williams wrested the title from McConachy and went on to beat off four challenges – Bernard Bennett in 1971, Jack Karnhem in 1973, and Eddie Charlton in 1974 and 1976 – before losing the crown to Fred Davis in 1980. The event became a knockout tournament that year, and Rex was twice the winner of the new-style competition, in 1982 and 1983, thereby confirming his expertise at the three-ball game.

Thanks to Rex Williams again, snooker's professional body was resurrected in 1969, and the World Championship reverted to the knockout format. Despite his efforts in promoting the Championship, Williams himself never subsequently appeared in the world final. The nearest he came was in 1969, 1972 and 1974, when John Spencer, Alex Higgins and Graham Miles respectively ended his chances. In the 1972 semi-final, Williams led Alex Higgins by six frames at one stage before losing 31–30.

In the qualifying round of the 1978 UK Snooker Championships, Williams trailed 8–2 to Terry Griffiths before taking seven frames in succession to win 9–8. An identical score, but this time against him, saw him exit the competition at the hands of Graham Miles. However, the UK Professional Billiards Championship, staged at the Northern Snooker Centre, Leeds, gave Williams the opportunity to exhibit his superior skills at the 'senior' game. The title had been held by Fred Davis for twenty-eight years, but in February 1979 Fred was a losing semi-finalist. Rex Williams became the new champion after beating John Barrie of Wisbech by 2,952 points to 2,116 in the final.

There followed a relatively lean period until the 1985–6 season brought about renewed confidence for Williams, then 51 years old. He reached the fourth round of the Rothman's Grand Prix, went one better in the Coral UK Open, and then reached the semi-final of the Mercantile Credit Classic, where he put up a great battle against Jimmy White. Ten ranking points that season elevated him into the top sixteen and the following season he improved three places after reaching his first ever ranking tournament final, the Rothman's Grand Prix. On his way to the final he beat Alex Higgins (5–1), Steve Davis (5–1) and Neal Foulds (9–8), but there was to be no fairy-tale ending, for, despite leading 5–2 at one stage, he went down 10–6 to Jimmy White. After that Rex slipped out of the top sixteen – and the troubled times at the WPBSA did not help.

Williams, who left his post as chairman of the WPBSA in 2000, then ran a lucrative pool and snooker-table manufacturing business for many years, which he operated from his Brierley Hill factory. The company, Rex Williams Leisure, was set up in 1975 and manufactured its own tables for hire to pubs and clubs up and down the country. In another capacity, he acted as a TV commentator, and in the rare intervals when he was not involved in billiards and snooker, he was a keen bird watcher – an interest he keeps up to this day.

World Professional Snooker Champions

Professional World Championship

1927	Joe Davis beat Tom Dennis	20–11
1928	Joe Davis beat Fred Lawrence	16–13
1929	Joe Davis beat Tom Dennis	19–14
1930	Joe Davis beat Tom Dennis	25–12
1931	Joe Davis beat Tom Dennis	25–21
1932	Joe Davis beat Clark McConachy	30–19
1933	Joe Davis beat Willie Smith	25–18
1934	Joe Davis beat Tom Newman	25–23
1935	Joe Davis beat Willie Smith	25–20
1936	Joe Davis beat Horace Lindrum	34–27
1937	Joe Davis beat Horace Lindrum	32–29
1938	Joe Davis beat Sidney Smith	37–24
1939	Joe Davis beat Sidney Smith	43–30
1940	Joe Davis beat Fred Davis	37–36
1946	Joe Davis beat Horace Lindrum	78–67
1947	Walter Donaldson beat Fred Davis	82–63
1948	Fred Davis beat Walter Donaldson	84–61
1949	Fred Davis beat Walter Donaldson	80–65
1950	Walter Donaldson beat Fred Davis	51–46
1951	Fred Davis beat Walter Donaldson	58–39

Professional Match-Play Championship

1952	Fred Davis beat Walter Donaldson	38–35
1953	Fred Davis beat Walter Donaldson	37–34
1954	Fred Davis beat Walter Donaldson	39–21
1955	Fred Davis beat John Pulman	37–34
1956	Fred Davis beat John Pulman	38–35
1957	John Pulman beat Jack Rea	39–34

Through lack of public support no championship was organized between 1957 and 1964. After a truce with the Billiard Association and Control Council, a new system was adopted whereby the champion defended his title against a series of single challengers.

Challenge Matches

1964	John Pulman beat Fred Davis	19–16
	John Pulman beat Rex Williams	40–33
1965	John Pulman beat Fred Davis	37–36
	John Pulman beat Rex Williams	25–22
	John Pulman beat Jimmy van Rensburg	39–12
1966	John Pulman beat Fred Davis	5–2 (matches)
1967	No challenge offered	
1968	John Pulman beat Eddie Charlton	39–34

Professional Open Championship

1969	John Spencer beat Gary Owen	37–24
1970	Ray Reardon beat John Pulman	37–33
1971	John Spencer beat Warren Simpson	37–29
1972	Alex Higgins beat John Spencer	37–32
1973	Ray Reardon beat Eddie Charlton	38–32
1974	Ray Reardon beat Graham Miles	22–12
1975	Ray Reardon beat Eddie Charlton	31–30

Embassy World Professional Open Championship

1976	Ray Reardon beat Alex Higgins	27–16
1977	John Spencer beat Cliff Thorburn	25–21
1978	Ray Reardon beat Perrie Mans	25–18
1979	Terry Griffiths beat Dennis Taylor	24–16
1980	Cliff Thorburn beat Alex Higgins	18–16
1981	Steve Davis beat Doug Mountjoy	18–12
1982	Alex Higgins beat Ray Reardon	18–15
1983	Steve Davis beat Cliff Thorburn	18–6
1984	Steve Davis beat Jimmy White	18–16
1985	Dennis Taylor beat Steve Davis	18–17
1986	Joe Johnson beat Steve Davis	18–12
1987	Steve Davis beat Joe Johnson	18–14
1988	Steve Davis beat Terry Griffiths	18–11
1989	Steve Davis beat John Parrott	18–3
1990	Stephen Hendry beat Jimmy White	18–12
1991	John Parrott beat Jimmy White	18–11
1992	Stephen Hendry beat Jimmy White	18–14
1993	Stephen Hendry beat Jimmy White	18–5

1994	Stephen Hendry beat Jimmy White	18–17
1995	Stephen Hendry beat Nigel Bond	18–9
1996	Stephen Hendry beat Peter Ebdon	18–12
1997	Ken Doherty beat Stephen Hendry	18–12
1998	John Higgins beat Ken Doherty	18–12
1999	Stephen Hendry beat Mark Williams	18–11
2000	Mark Williams beat Matthew Stevens	18–16
2001	Ronnie O'Sullivan beat John Higgins	18–14
2002	Peter Ebdon beat Stephen Hendry	18–17
2003	Mark Williams beat Ken Doherty	18–16

Acknowledgements

The author would like to thank the following organizations for their help in the compilation of this book: The World Professional Billiards and Snooker Association, and Snooker Scene. Also the following individuals: Ben Hayes, Peter Constable, Mark Griffiths and Mark Edwards of Eddie's Snooker Club, Haverfordwest. Also, of course, my thanks go to Terry Griffiths for writing the foreword to the book.

Picture Credits

The photographs in this book have come from the *Lancashire Evening Post*, with the exception of those on pp. 13, 23, 29, 43, 57, 64, 83, 89, 101, 105, 121, 123, 128 and 130, which come from the Eric Whitehead collection.